TO SAVE
EVERY ONE

TO SAVE EVERY ONE

Lifeboats

with Sarah Thompson

HarperCollins*Publishers*

CONTENTS

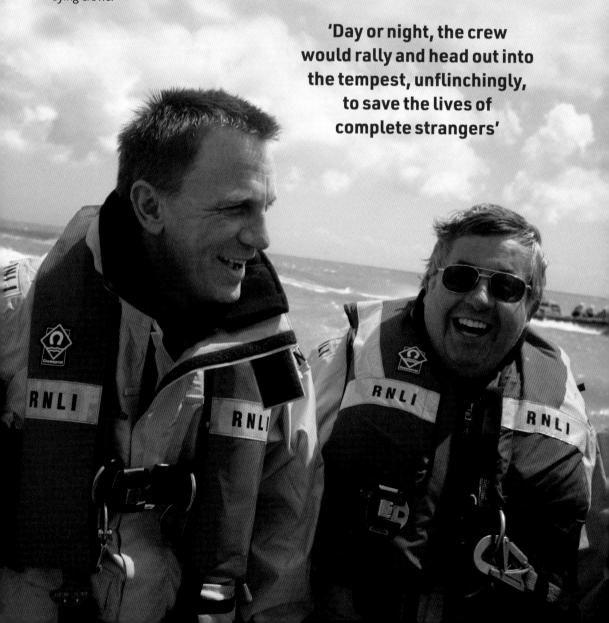

FOREWORD

Every child who grows up on the Wirral is taught very early on that a peninsula is a body of land almost completely surrounded by water. The sea becomes an intrinsic part of your life: the Mersey to the north and east, with the old Liverpool docks and their complicated, rich history, alongside the great expanse of the Dee estuary to the south and west, where I spent nearly every day of my childhood beachcombing and dreaming. Then there's the Irish Sea: beautiful, ever-changing, and sometimes deeply treacherous. Some winters the gale-force winds seemed unceasing, with cars in the street lifting off their axles and slates from roofs spiralling to the ground like dying crows.

PHOTO: Greg Williams

'Day or night, the crew
would rally and head out into
the tempest, unflinchingly,
to save the lives of
complete strangers'

Hoylake RNLI volunteers bringing their lifeboat *Mary Gabriel* back to the station after a launch in bitterly cold conditions. The lifeboat served from 1974–1990.

What you got used to very quickly, growing up next to an RNLI station, was the sound of the signal flare going up, a loud percussive noise that either indicated a drill or, more often – when the sea was at its most violent – a full-on emergency. Day or night, the crew would rally and head out into the tempest, unflinchingly, to save the lives of complete strangers, over and over again.

My admiration for the crews and all the support teams of the incredible RNLI is boundless. Our coastline defines the nation; it's in our DNA. What the RNLI does 24 hours a day, 365 days a year, is keep us connected to it: giving safe passage to trade routes, the fishing fleet and those seeking pleasure on the high seas.

The tragedy of Penlee and the *Solomon Browne*, along with many others, is never forgotten. The sacrifice of those crews is burnt indelibly into the history of the RNLI, but so too is the almost daily occurrence of survival and selfless heroism that makes this extraordinary organisation what it is: safely returning those in peril to their loved ones.

It is an honour and very humbling to write this foreword, and I encourage you to support these brave, wonderful people in any way you can.

'With courage, nothing is impossible.'
Long live the RNLI.

Daniel Craig

ONE MAN, ONE VISION
How the RNLI began

1

For 200 years people have counted on the RNLI to keep them safe on, in and next to the water. Since then, the charity has saved an estimated 150,000 lives and kept many more from harm through its safety work. Today the charity still depends on volunteers and donors to power its vision: to save every one. But whose idea was it to start the world's first sea-rescue charity? And where did it begin?

Shipwreck: a part of life

The grim sight of battered shipwrecks and news of lost crews were only too common around the British coastline in the 18th century. They were a part of life. Some ports and towns had their own lifeboats on hand to answer the call for help, but building lifeboats was an expensive task and not every community had a wealthy benefactor to pay for one.

Sir William Hillary was an experienced sailor who had once been a wealthy man. But he had fallen into debt and in 1808 he fled England to live on the Isle of Man. While there he witnessed several shipping disasters in Douglas Bay and decided he could not stand by while lives were being lost at sea.

In October 1822 he joined a rescue effort to save the crew of a Royal Navy cutter in a gale.

Sir William Hillary, founder of the RNLI.

Using rowing boats, he and his fellow rescuers (mostly naval crew) pulled the listing cutter clear from rocks and returned safely to shore. Following this, Hillary helped Douglas volunteers save more vessels, towing them from danger and hauling them to the beach. Although they saved many lives, it was dangerous work aboard simple boats – and most of the local men, who had families and livelihoods to keep, had been reluctant to volunteer.

Hillary's experiences led him to use his connections and call upon some of the most influential people of the time to help him form a national institution that would preserve human life from shipwreck. He printed and distributed an appeal leaflet in 1823. 'On some occasions, it has been my lot to witness the loss of many valuable lives,' it read, 'under circumstances where, had there been establishments already formed for affording prompt relief, and encouragement given to those who might volunteer on such a cause, in all probability the greater part would have been rescued from destruction.'

Fellow creatures in peril

At the heart of this institution would be 'a large body of men ... in constant readiness to risk their own lives for the preservation of those whom they have never known or seen, perhaps of another nation, merely because they are fellow creatures in extreme peril'.

The priorities of the institution would include 'the preservation of human life from shipwreck ... assistance to vessels in distress ... support of those persons who may be rescued'. But Hillary's noble idea was ignored at first – the Admiralty refused to help. Hillary refused to give up, however.

'Although they saved many lives, it was dangerous work aboard simple boats'

Instead, he rebranded his appeal, this time aiming it at the more philanthropic members of London society. And it worked. Benefactors came onboard, in particular Thomas Wilson, the energetic Liberal MP for Southwark, and shipping magnate George Hibbert, the Whig MP for Seaford and Chairman of the West India Merchants Society. Despite some personal differences, the three men became a formidable force and the campaign rapidly gathered momentum. In time, more and more benefactors joined the cause, inspired by the idea they might help save lives.

The City of London Tavern in Bishopsgate, where the original RNLI was formed. More than 30 aristocrats, clerics, politicians, naval officers, brokers, bankers, merchants and philanthropists put their names to the fledgling RNLI at the public meeting. King George IV granted the Royal prefix to the Institution's name, making it the Royal National Institution for the Preservation of Life from Shipwreck. On 5 October 1854, the Institution's name was changed to the Royal National Lifeboat Institution – the RNLI.

Frontispiece to European Magazine. *VOL.55.*

Engraved by Roorke, from a drawing by S. Shepherd.

THE CITY OF LONDON TAVERN.
Bishopsgate Street.
Published by J. Asperne, at the Bible, Crown & Constitution, Cornhill, February 1.1809.

More than 30 eminent gentlemen put their names to the fledgling RNLI at the inaugural public meeting. Prime Minister Robert Jenkinson, 2nd Earl of Liverpool, agreed to be President, while Vice President Dr Charles Manners-Sutton, the Archbishop of Canterbury, presided over the meeting. And among the aristocrats, clerics, politicians, naval officers, brokers, bankers, merchants and philanthropists were William Wilberforce and sea-safety guru Captain George Manby.

For more information on how the RNLI was founded and funded, visit RNLI.org/foundation

Timeless commitment

When the RNLI was formed, 12 resolutions were passed, including:

That an Institution can now be formed ... to be supported by donations and annual subscriptions.

That such immediate assistance be afforded to persons rescued as their necessities may require.

After establishing a UK-based lifeguard service in 2001, the RNLI went on to help other lifesaving organisations set up their own lifeguard services – including the teams at Cox's Bazar in Bangladesh, the world's longest natural sea beach (pictured).

That the subjects of all nations be equally objects of the Institution, as well in war as in peace ...

The RNLI is playing a key role in helping to tackle the international drowning epidemic.

They could not have known at the time that these 12 resolutions would still stand as part of the RNLI's charter 200 years later. A further nine resolutions, mainly recognising the efforts of the key players, were also met with eager approval. It was a landmark moment for Sir William Hillary, who became known as the 'Father of the Institution'. His vision had finally become a reality. King George lV became Patron and granted permission for the Royal prefix to the institution's name, making it the Royal National Institution for the Preservation of Life from Shipwreck.

Two months after the original RNLI was formed, Sir William Hillary wrote:

'This Institution has been [honoured] by the high patronage of the King … sanctioned by many of the most distinguished characters in the church and state, and sustained by the bounty of a generous nation. It only remains for me to express the heartfelt satisfaction … that this Institution is now established on principles which will extend its beneficial effects to the most distant shores, and to generations yet unborn.'

A lifesaving legacy

The RNLI began to provide lifeboats to areas that needed them, including the Isle of Man, where Hillary returned to live out his days. He led many lifesaving rescues there over the following years, aboard the lifeboats provided by the institution he had proudly founded. He died on 5 January 1847, aged 76. His tomb in St George's churchyard in Douglas bears the inscription of the RNLI and his image is still shown on all RNLI Medals for Gallantry.

Today, as we celebrate 200 years since the institution began, his lifesaving legacy continues around the coast and inland, with lifeboat crews, lifeguards and water safety work keeping thousands of people safe every year around the UK, Ireland and beyond.

'With courage, nothing is impossible'
SIR WILLIAM HILLARY

16 | ON.927

RNLB GRACE DARLING
35FT 6IN LIVERPOOL CLASS TWIN SCREW LIFEBOAT (1954-84)

Lifeboats

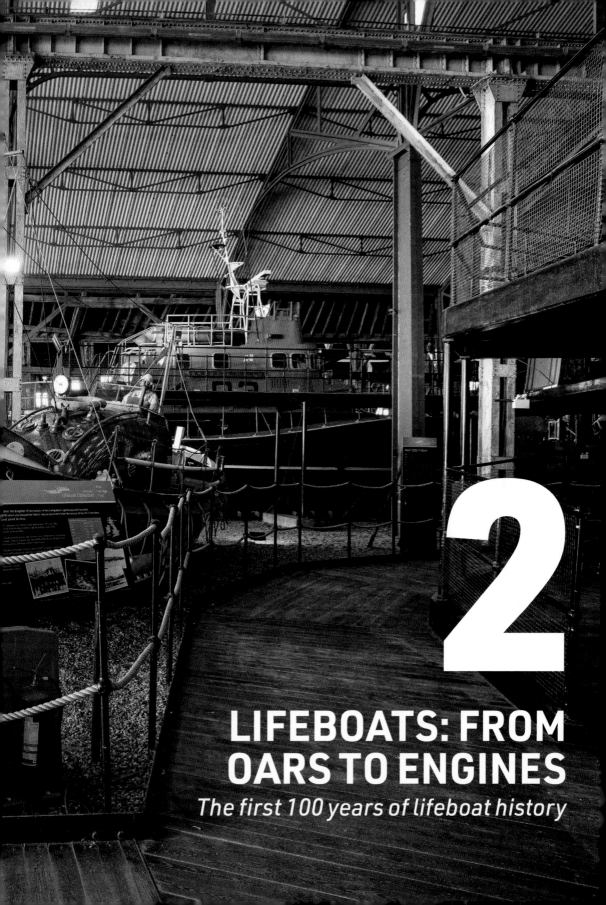

2

LIFEBOATS: FROM OARS TO ENGINES

The first 100 years of lifeboat history

By the time the Royal National Institution for the Preservation of Life from Shipwreck was founded in 1824 there were already a number of different lifeboats in service at locations around the coast of the UK. For many decades coastal communities had been pulling together in their own ways to help those involved in shipwrecks, and many had local boats and systems for when help was needed. But when the first purpose-built lifeboat came to be and precisely who invented it remain disputed issues among lifeboat historians.

The first lifeboat?

A Londoner, Lionel Lukin, may have conceived the first purpose-built lifeboat when he designed an unsinkable boat and patented it on 2 November 1785. Although a coachbuilder by trade, Lukin had always been interested in improving the safety of boats, and in 1784 he began experimenting with a Norwegian yawl, a type of sailing boat. Using the River Thames to test his 'unimmergible' design, Lukin incorporated pockets of air in watertight compartments, buoyant gunwales, cork and other light materials in the structure. He also included a false iron keel for additional weight to help keep the boat upright.

Lukin's design was so successful that the following year he was commissioned to convert a coble, a type of fishing boat, into an 'unimmergible' boat for the people of Bamburgh in Northumberland. This boat was in service for a number of years as a dedicated lifeboat. During storms, men from Bamburgh Castle patrolled the shores on horseback, ready to go to sea in their lifeboat and help save lives from shipwreck. So Lukin's boat can in theory claim to be the first lifeboat, and Bamburgh Castle the first lifeboat station.

But Lukin's converted coble did not lead to any further commissions of the same type, and it wasn't until 1789 that the private Law House committee in nearby South Shields commenced its search for an inventor who could construct a purpose-built lifeboat. The search was triggered by a tragedy at the mouth of the River Tyne. England's north-east was at that time already a world-renowned maritime hub, with a thriving shipbuilding industry and a busy seafaring coastline. A ship named *Adventure* ran aground during a violent storm, but the sea was so rough that local men and their boats couldn't reach the crew of the ship. Instead, crowds had to stand by and watch as *Adventure*'s crew drowned.

Henry Greathead, builder of the pioneering *Original* lifeboat.

Two great minds: Wouldhave and Greathead

The committee's competition offered a prize of two guineas for the best design and, among the many entries, two stood out. Parish clerk William Wouldhave and local boatbuilder Henry Francis Greathead, both from South Shields, submitted designs that caught the committee's attention.

Wouldhave's innovative design was for a boat made out of copper and cork that would right itself in stormy seas. Greathead's model was built out of wood, and although it had some excellent features it didn't self-right like Wouldhave's design. Seeing potential in both men's ideas, the committee declared that neither design was an outright winner but instead took elements from both offerings to produce a prototype for a final lifeboat design.

Wouldhave took offence at this idea and, despite being offered half of the prize money as a reward, rejected it. So the committee turned to Greathead – the more experienced boatbuilder – and asked him to build the lifeboat from the final design. Greathead's resulting boat was named the *Original*, and he has come to be known as the inventor of the lifeboat, although in truth the earlier work of both Wouldhave and Lukin contributed to Greathead's design. Perhaps in acknowledgement of this, Greathead never took out a patent on his lifeboat, and was always willing to share his plans for the good of others and saving lives at sea.

A model of the *Original*, Henry Greathead's lifeboat built in South Shields in 1789.

FOCUS ON: THE *ORIGINAL*

What were the features that made Greathead's *Original* lifeboat so different from the regular rowing boats that had been used until then?

The first *Original* was stationed at South Shields and kept in a boathouse close to the beach. When the lifeboat was needed, a boy paraded the streets banging a drum to let the local men know someone was in danger. It was launched with a wheeled carriage that had to be hauled over the beach by locals and sometimes a team of horses. Its first rescue was on 30 January 1790, when the lifeboat volunteers saved a shipwrecked crew on Herd Sand. Henry Greathead went on to build 31 *Original*-type lifeboats over the next two decades for maritime communities at home and abroad.

could be rowed in either direction thanks to the lack of a rudder

9m long and 3m wide

room for 20 people, including a crew of up to 12

curved keel for easier steering

short oars for better manageability in choppy waters

sides cased with cork and copper plates to increase buoyancy

Zetland: the oldest lifeboat

The oldest surviving *Original*-type lifeboat, *Zetland*, was built by Greathead in 1802 and is now on public display at the Zetland Lifeboat Museum in Redcar. It was used to save over 500 lives at sea off the notoriously treacherous Redcar coast. In 1864, when the new lifeboat *Crossley* arrived at Redcar, *Zetland* was hauled to the beach and an RNLI joiner was ordered to destroy it. The people of Redcar objected and it was agreed that *Zetland* would remain in the care of the town. The lifeboat was then managed locally and was even used for rescue as late as 1880, 78 years after being built. *Zetland* has remained in Redcar ever since, and is listed on the UK's National Register of Historic Vessels, as part of the nation's historic fleet.

We are sailing

In 1851, recognising that the existing lifeboat fleet was aging and, in some locations, limited by its one-size-fits-all design, the institution launched another competition to design a new lifeboat. This time the contest's results were showcased at the Great Exhibition of the Works of Industry of All Nations, also known as the Great Exhibition, at the Crystal Palace in London. There was a prize of 100 guineas, offered by the President of the Institution, the Duke of Northumberland, and almost 300 entries came from all over the world. The top 50 designs were displayed in the palace for visitors to see, attracting much attention and helping to publicise the Institution's work.

The award for the best design went to the shipwright James Beeching. His boat was 36 feet long, was pulled with 12 oars and was the first lifeboat to be rigged with sails. It was also the first self-righting lifeboat, something made possible by a heavy iron keel, huge air cases and a heavy water ballast.

Adding sails to lifeboats was an important stage in their development – in the right conditions, crews could use lifeboats like *St Paul* (pictured) to go further and faster.

See it in real life
The *St Paul* lifeboat, built in 1897, is on display at the Historic Dockyard in Chatham, Kent. It is part of the RNLI's Historic Lifeboat Collection, where visitors can see all sorts of legendary lifesaving craft and explore interactive displays, archive film and audio clips.

From rowing, to sailing, to steaming: *Duke of Northumberland* was the first steam-powered RNLI lifeboat.

As with the approach of the committee in 1789, the judges saw Beeching's boat not as the ultimate in lifeboat design, but instead as a starting point from which more could be achieved. Various versions of Beeching's sail lifeboat were commissioned, each one specifically adapted to suit the challenges of the local geography, so different types of lifeboats began to operate from coastal locations around the country.

Perhaps the most successful of these was an adaptation of Beeching's design by the master shipwright James Peake. He took Beeching's prototype and created a lighter – and cheaper to build – model that was made out of copper-fastened elm. Peake's boat was popular with lifeboat crews because it was so much easier to handle. This model came to be known as the Beeching-Peake and was the workhorse of the RNLI for the next 30 or so years.

'This model ... was the workhorse of the RNLI'

Steaming ahead

By the late 19th century, steam had transformed the UK's industrial landscape. Steamships and steam-powered railways were driving huge growth and progress in almost every aspect of life. The RNLI's pulling (rowing) and sailing lifeboats continued to save lives at sea, but were limited in their scope, especially in heavy seas. Could steam power and modern technology transform the RNLI's lifeboats in the way it had other forms of transport?

Tending a coal-fired boiler in a boat that is pitching and rolling in heavy seas would not turn out to be straightforward. *Duke of Northumberland*, the RNLI's first steam-cum-sail boat, entered service at Harwich Lifeboat Station in Essex, in September 1890. The hydraulic steam-driven lifeboat used waterjets instead of propellers and was based on an 1888 scale model built by Greens of Blackwall.

The charity commissioned five further steam-driven lifeboats; two used waterjets, while the others were propeller-driven. Together, these lifeboats were in service for over 40 years and saved almost 600 lives but they were slow, heavy and expensive to maintain. When the steam-driven lifeboat *James Stevens No. 4* was wrecked at Padstow in Cornwall in 1900 with the loss of eight crew, it marked the beginning of the end for steam, and no more steam-driven RNLI lifeboats were ever built.

Petrol power

The earliest petrol-driven lifeboats were adaptations of existing pulling and sailing ones. Petrol had proven its prowess in the motorcar and the aeroplane, but petrol and seawater were as yet unacquainted, and making an engine casing that was watertight but not airtight would be one of the greatest challenges for boatbuilders of the era. Naval architect George Lennox Watson successfully fitted a petrol engine into an RNLI sailing lifeboat and trialled it in the Solent in 1904, but lifeboat crews everywhere were largely unimpressed by the idea of a motorised lifeboat. That reluctance, combined with costs and the First World War, meant that progression towards more petrol power was slow.

At the start of the 20th century, the RNLI's Naval Architect George Lennox Watson created the charity's first petrol-powered craft by fitting an engine to a sailing lifeboat.

Henry Vernon: The one that swung it

A year later, to a lukewarm reception from the unenthusiastic crew, the first petrol-driven lifeboat – *J McConnell Hussey* – entered service at Tynemouth Lifeboat Station in north-east England. Although motorised lifeboats continued to be viewed with suspicion, the station's second petrol-driven lifeboat, *Henry Vernon*, would change the story of lifesaving forever in 1914 when it was called upon to help reach survivors from the hospital steamship *Rohilla*.

The ship – a converted pleasure cruiser – was on its way to Dunkirk on a mission to bring back wounded British soldiers from the war. Its passengers were ambulance crew, nurses and doctors, all preparing themselves for the horrors of the front line. But *Rohilla* never made it to France. Instead it hit heavy seas off the coast of Whitby, around 40 miles south of Tynemouth, and smashed into a reef. *Rohilla* immediately snapped in two, and half of the ship and its passengers were lost to the sea. The challenge for Whitby's lifesavers was now to save as many as they could from what remained of *Rohilla*.

From propellers to waterjets. Discover how lifeboats evolved in the 20th century on page 154.

LEFT: Coxswain Robert Smith led the Tynemouth crew to the rescue aboard the *Henry Vernon* motor lifeboat.

BELOW: Volunteers struggled to rescue *Rohilla's* crew using rowing lifeboats like the *William Riley* (pictured being recovered).

Whitby's RNLI volunteers tried valiantly to reach *Rohilla*, but the seas were vicious and their lifeboat *John Fielden* took some damaging hits as the crew rowed tirelessly to reach the wreck against the lurching swells of the storm. They managed to save 23 passengers before the lifeboat failed in the gale and became unseaworthy. Hearing of *Rohilla* and how their fellow lifeboat volunteers were struggling to complete the rescue, the Tynemouth crew assembled in *Henry Vernon* and sped south to the wreck, where, after almost three days, around 50 survivors still clung to the stricken ship.

The nimble, motor-powered *Henry Vernon* was able to get alongside the sinking *Rohilla*, just as it looked as though all hope was lost. More than 140 people were rescued, including the ship's captain and his cat, in no small part thanks to the fast response of the motorised lifeboat.

Those who had initially doubted the benefits of motor-powered boats could no longer deny the value of this type of lifeboat and, with that, the RNLI's capacity for lifesaving was revolutionised.

LEFT: The RNLI's motor lifeboat *Henry Vernon* and her crew, who were instrumental in the rescue of the *Rohilla*.

RIGHT: This RNLI poster from the late 1920s included a map of stationed lifeboats.

'Those who had initially doubted the benefits of motor power could no longer deny the value of this type of lifeboat'

VALIANT VOLUNTEERS

*The RNLI relies on thousands of volunteers
to power its lifesaving service – people like
you who help in all sorts of ways*

3

Everyone who lends their time, passion and talent to the RNLI is helping to save lives – you don't have to be a lifeguard or lifeboat crew member to make a difference. There are lots of ways to volunteer, from being a press officer at your local station or a sales assistant in the shop, to educating kids and sharing your business experience. We are lucky that thousands of people with specific skills and experience give their time to help us across the UK and Ireland.

PREVIOUS PAGE: RNLI volunteers find all sorts of ways to save lives with their time and talent – like Clogherhead's Lifeboat Choir.

The shop volunteer

Rosie Fisher gives her time at RNLI Barry Island Visitor Centre in Glamorgan – an attraction on the seafront that shares safety advice through fun activities and displays. There's also a fundraising shop at the centre, which Rosie helps to run. 'It's important to me because I know I'm doing something useful and worthwhile. The RNLI is a charity and wouldn't survive without its fundraisers and shop volunteers. I never get that Monday morning feeling of not wanting to go to the shop. I always look forward to it!'

The fundraiser

Nicola Barker-Harrison is the RNLI Branch Secretary at Kinghorn, Fife. 'When it comes to our fundraising events I help with everything, from liaising with the other emergency services before our annual open day and doing risk assessments to sending out thank you letters after an event,' explains Nicola. 'Plus I'll do whatever else needs doing on the day, whether that's flipping burgers or painting children's faces!

'Volunteering is a team effort and my team are brilliant. We all have a good laugh together. I've got to know them so well and we've become firm friends. And, by being involved, I'm helping to make sure we do all we can to save every one, not just people where I live.

'For most volunteer roles you don't need any prior experience. You just need to be willing to give things a shot when you're asked, and to try your best. There's something for everybody. I'd say if you're thinking about volunteering, even just a little bit, give it a shot. You'll have a good time and you'll feel a little bit better about yourself too.'

Find out more about our fundraising efforts and the incredible amounts people have raised for the RNLI on page 66.

The lifeboat operations manager

Shawna Johnson plays a vital lifesaving role from the shore at Kilrush in County Clare. Every lifeboat station has an operations manager who carries out the day-to-day management of the lifeboat station to ensure the crews are always ready for service. When the call comes in from the Coast Guard requesting the lifeboat's help, Shawna authorises the crew launch and alerts the volunteers. 'My job is to support the crew and the station, and to keep a cool head while doing it,' she explains. 'I'm always looking ahead; you can never rest on your laurels. What happens next? What do our people need to do their job? How can we get new people involved and how do we keep our community safe on the water? I run a pub, so I'm used to being busy and getting stuck in – I don't know any other way. I love it.'

The museum curator

Neil Williamson is the volunteer curator of the museum at Whitby Lifeboat Station in North Yorkshire. When the former boathouse was relocated in 1958, the original building became the museum, one of the RNLI's most visited and successful. As well as featuring artefacts and records of the station's gallantry, the collection at Whitby is dedicated to one of the RNLI's oldest rowing lifeboats, the 104-year-old *Robert and Ellen Robson*, whose restoration Neil helped to oversee in 2022.

As well as welcoming visitors and coordinating the team of volunteers, Neil takes care of the historic building and other displays. He says: 'I love being the museum curator. I've been a crew member in the past and have a love of history, so it all ties in nicely with the role. The RNLI has so many interesting stories of heroism and courage that need to be recorded and passed on to future generations.'

The trustee

Jim Islam is an RNLI trustee and in 2022 became the charity's treasurer, overseeing the financial performance of the entire organisation. Being a trustee – as the name implies – requires an immense amount of trust and care. It means taking responsibility for the RNLI's activities, and ensuring that it is working genuinely and solely in pursuit of its lifesaving objectives. Jim is a qualified actuary with over 20 years' leadership experience in the insurance, investment management, savings and pensions sectors. He says: 'I feel privileged to be part of the RNLI, an institution that reflects the best values of our communities, with courageous and inspiring people achieving marvellous feats.'

PREVIOUS PAGE: Volunteers are crucial when it comes to saving lives through water safety education. See Chapter 10 for more on the RNLI's work with children and young people.

The one of a kind

Mary Taylor was an integral part of Padstow RNLI, Cornwall, for the best part of a century. Known to many as Lifeboat Mary, she was from a long line of RNLI volunteers. Her father and grandfather were coxswains, one uncle was the mechanic and one uncle was the winchman. Mary started collecting for the lifeboats when she was a little girl, and as she grew up she began to cook hearty breakfasts for the crew when they came back in from a shout. A talented embroiderer, she made pictures of every Padstow lifeboat and these still hang in the boathouse. Her embroidery became so popular that an embroidered tablecloth set with six serviettes and a tray cloth was raffled off for over £12,000, paying for a lift at the station to help the crew get up and down the cliff.

As well as knitting and baking for fundraising events, Mary made endless cups of tea for the crew, and her picture even made it onto the official packaging of our own Lifeboat Tea, profits from the sales of which went to the RNLI. When asked what her favourite thing about the RNLI was, Mary said it was the lifeboat crew members. 'They're so wonderful. I'd do anything for them. I always stand at the door and say: "Safe passage, my darlings. Give me a shout when you're back."'

Mary died aged 84 in 2015, and it's estimated she raised over £70,000 for the RNLI in her lifetime.

FOCUS ON: HOW YOUR TIME AND TALENTS COULD SAVE LIVES

If you're reading this and wondering how you can help, here are a few other things people do to support us.

Promote the RNLI
Be a visits guide at your local station or give talks at your local community centre, yacht club or business groups.

Volunteer in our offices
You could bring your expertise to a specific project or by providing administrative support to teams throughout the organisation.

Share the RNLI's history
Welcome people to an RNLI museum or visitor centre – or give your time as a remote volunteer for the RNLI Heritage Team.

Cheer us on
Fundraisers who are competing in races or taking on big challenges always need support. If you haven't got much time but you can wave a flag and cheer enthusiastically, this is a great way to help.

The RNLI wouldn't be able to show its work and history to visitors of all ages without the volunteers who give tours and talks at our stations and other buildings – including Barry Island Visitor Centre, pictured.

Head to an RNLI event and you might bump into our well-loved mascot Stormy Stan – another crucial volunteer role.

Be a street collector

Street collections are still at the heart of what we do. You can help raise money for the RNLI by volunteering to collect at an organised street collection.

Be a lifeboat station or lifeguard volunteer

Are you ready to give up your time to train for lifesaving rescues and carry them out? We depend on volunteers to launch and crew lifeboats – plus some lifeguard patrols need volunteers too.

Spread our safety messages

Whether they give talks to schools or yacht clubs, water safety volunteers are lifesavers in their own right – and we need more!

Share our messages

Publicity helps raise crucial RNLI funds and awareness. Your local lifeboat station might need your PR skills as a volunteer press officer. Or you can tell our stories simply by following us on social media and sharing RNLI posts. This takes no time and makes a big difference. You'll find the RNLI on Facebook, Instagram, LinkedIn, TikTok, X (formerly Twitter) and YouTube.

For more on volunteering opportunities with the RNLI, visit RNLI.org/volunteer.

4

TRAINED TO BE READY
FOR ANYTHING

*From the deep end to the front line – how do
volunteer crews build their lifesaving skills?*

Every RNLI lifeboat crew member goes through some of the world's best and most rigorous lifesaving training. By the time they launch on their first rescue, they will have received training in using their kit, their lifeboat's layout and what to do in an emergency.

But crew training wasn't always like this. When the first fishermen and sailors who became the earliest registered crew members headed out in heavy wooden lifeboats to save those in need, they'd had next to no training for the job. It helped that many of them were already from seafaring communities and accustomed to life on the waves – they understood the water and its dangers. Many, however, were still not familiar with the other vital aspects of lifesaving, such as the early recognition of certain serious conditions or the correct way to handle broken bones. Far less was known about the human body and its care in an emergency.

An extract from an article titled 'Directions for Restoring the Apparently Drowned', from the *Lifeboat* journal of May 1882.

Excite the nostrils with snuff, hartshorn, and smelting salts, or tickle the throat with a feather, &c., if they are at hand. Rub the chest and face warm, and dash cold water, or cold and hot water alternately on them. If there be no success, lose not a moment, but instantly—

To Imitate Breathing—Replace the patient on the face, raising and supporting the chest well on a folded coat or other article of dress.

Turn the body very gently on the side and a little beyond, and then briskly on the face, back again, repeating these measures cautiously, efficiently, and perseveringly, about fifteen times in the minute, or once every four or five seconds, occasionally varying the side.

'Far less was known about the human body and its care in an emergency'

So how did the RNLI's training become the world-class programme our crews complete today? And what exactly does going through that process entail?

Early training

'Send immediately for medical assistance, blankets, and dry clothing, but proceed to treat the Patient instantly on the spot, in the open air, with the face downward, whether on shore or afloat; exposing the face, neck, and chest to the wind, except in severe weather, and removing all tight clothing from the neck and chest, especially the braces.'

These lifesaving instructions were shared in an issue of the *Lifeboat* journal and are some of the earliest evidence of what we now know as lifesaving training. The journal says they were the result of 'extensive inquiries which were made by the Institution in 1863–4 amongst Medical Men, Medical Bodies, and Coroners throughout the United Kingdom'.

Among other advice in past *Lifeboat* journals is the suggestion that lifesavers could use a feather to tickle the throat of someone who is unconscious, and a warning that under no circumstances should a body be held upside down to revive it. There's also plenty of advice about the use of alcohol, which was kept on lifeboats until the mid-20th century. A passage from a *Lifeboat* journal of 1915 describes how the crew was absolutely not permitted to drink the stores of alcohol when the sun was shining:

'The spirits carried in Life-boats are always to be kept locked up in the provision box or locker fitted in the boat, and the Coxswain is to keep the keys. They [the spirits] are primarily intended for any persons rescued from a wreck who may be in a dangerous state of collapse from cold, exposure, or want of food. The Crew are on no account to partake of the spirits in summer, or on short services in winter when the weather is mild.'

'Degenerate into loafers'

The introduction of motorised lifeboats in the early 20th century meant that there was less need for crew members to have a maritime background, although many still did come from the fishing and boating communities where the lifeboats were needed most. An issue of the *Lifeboat* journal from 1916 tells how the idea of recruiting men from non-maritime backgrounds would almost certainly lead to grave problems:

'FROM time immemorial it has been the custom of the Life-boat Service not to maintain fixed crews for Life-boats, but to draw volunteers as required from the seafaring population of the coast towns and villages where Life-boats are stationed ... as the men, continuing to pursue their avocations as fishermen, boatmen, etc., and spending their lives in open boats, are kept in constant training for the particular class of work which is required in the Life-boat Service, the very nature of which is such that the occasions of use are few and far between; and a crew of men who did no other work would, it is feared, soon degenerate into loafers.'

Drawings and instructions from the *Lifeboat* journals in the early 20th century show how a crew member's understanding of the human body and how to treat those who have apparently drowned became more detailed. With greater medical training and the growing expectations of what a lifesaver could achieve in a rescue situation, the role of crew member was becoming more layered and complex than ever before.

Training today

Today, our crew members come from a wide range of backgrounds, with only around 10% being from the seafaring population that first made up our crews. Regardless of their experience and careers outside of the RNLI, every volunteer who joins now follows a structured and detailed crew-development plan in order to become a lifesaver. Every crew has weekly training, based at the station. These sessions take place at sea and ashore, with exercises focusing on everything from teamwork and technical competence to safe operating procedures and handling the lifeboat. Crew learn search and rescue techniques, navigation, radar training, radio communications and casualty care. Working alongside their fellow crew members, they also practise rescue scenarios involving other emergency services such as the Coastguard and Police.

The RNLI College's training facilities include a simulator that gives crews training in navigation, search patterns and leadership.

Volunteers must also understand the work that goes on in the background of any crew, be it the work of the lifeboat operations manager, the lifeboat press officer or the mechanic. It's important that every crew member is aware of every role and responsibility at the lifeboat station, that they know how to use and look after their personal protective equipment, learn the layout of their station's lifeboat, and understand how to use the equipment onboard and how to work with ropes safely. Every crew member starts off as crew and can go on – if they wish and a need arises – to take on more specialised roles, such as navigator, helm or coxswain.

Back to college

After months of initial training – and getting to know and work with their local crews – all trainees will attend the Crew Emergency Procedures course at the RNLI College in Poole, Dorset.

This course is where our trainees learn how to handle some of the most difficult situations in some of the most challenging conditions. Training exercises take place in the Sea Survival Centre, where state-of-the-art training equipment includes a wave tank to mimic heavy seas. It all provides the opportunity for trainees to learn how to deal with an emergency in more perilous conditions such as darkness, thunder and lightning, storms and heavy rain.

The RNLI College in Poole, Dorset, was opened in 2004. Having a dedicated college for crew training and development had long been a part of the RNLI's vision, and is a reflection of our ongoing commitment to crews and the high standards of training they receive. Find out more about the college and some of our stations and buildings on page 194.

Training continues

After completing their probationary period and assessments, trainees become fully fledged lifeboat crew members. But crew training never stops. Every crew member receives ongoing support and training on specialist courses run by trainers at the RNLI College or at their own stations.

The RNLI lifeboat Crew Emergency Procedures course includes an 'abandon ship' exercise, where trainees step off a 4m-high platform into the training pool.

'Big Sick, Little Sick'

Although the vast majority of RNLI volunteers join with no medical training, they're often required to treat casualties in demanding and stressful environments, from the deck of a lifeboat in a Force 9 gale to a busy beach. They therefore need to possess both the knowledge and the ability to assess the injury or illness and give vital first aid – doing so can mean the difference between life and death. So how do we ensure our crew members have the high standard of medical and emergency-care knowledge they need, and how do we help them get it quickly? Remembering the symptoms of numerous potential injuries or problems can take time that crew members on a rescue might not have, especially in the middle of the night in a storm.

Drawing on his own experience and knowledge of being on the crew, a volunteer crew member helped the RNLI develop a simple and effective solution to this challenge. To help volunteers easily work out the correct course of action to take, 'Big Sick, Little Sick' waterproof check cards were created.The cards enable crew members to treat a casualty quickly and correctly in the same time it would take to remember the difference

Tending to injured or ill people at sea or on the shoreline takes specialised training.

between the symptoms of a broken rib and those of tension pneumothorax. Using easy-to-read flow charts and questions, crew members can determine whether a casualty is 'Big Sick' – meaning that they are in serious danger and may die if they do not receive immediate medical attention – or 'Little Sick' – meaning they can still be in quite serious danger but are in a stable and non-critical condition.

These techniques have been widely praised by crew members for their accuracy, efficiency and simplicity.

RNLI lifeboat crew members and lifeguards are trained in casualty care using a 'Big Sick, Little Sick' system of check cards.

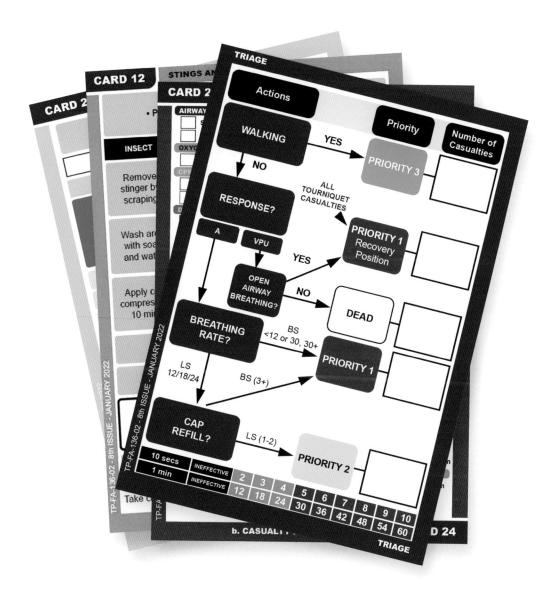

Support in tough times

Crew members' families, fellow volunteers and communities provide much-needed support to the lifesavers. And, while every crew member knows that challenging circumstances come with the role, the RNLI also recognises the huge impact being part of a lifeboat crew can have on emotional and mental wellbeing.

In 2016, the RNLI acted on the growing risk of potentially traumatic experiences in which our crew and lifeguards can find themselves. After running a pilot scheme in 2016, we established our TriM programme in 2018. TRiM stands for Trauma Risk Incident Management and it's a peer-led initiative, available to all of our lifeguards and crew members. TRiM is designed to help support any crew or lifeguards who have experienced a traumatic incident. If crews or lifeguards need to talk to someone, they can reach out to specially trained colleagues from other nearby lifeboat crews for help. We use psychological risk assessments similar to those used by the Royal Marines to assess a crew member or lifeguard's well-being, and if there is any concern we then make sure they get the right clinical help.

The considerable impact of being on a lifeboat crew reaches family members too. In 2015, the RNLI introduced the Families Programme as a way of acknowledging the sacrifices made, and support given, by families living with an RNLI pager in the household. It's a growing network of volunteers committed to improving their experience of being part of the RNLI family. A range of help is available, including support with station family events and access to RNLI support services in times of difficulty.

A key part of crew training is being ready for anything – even lifeboat capsize. Volunteers learn how to inflate and get aboard liferafts as part of their Crew Emergency Procedures course.

'Crew members' families, fellow volunteers and communities provide much-needed support to the lifesavers'

5

WOMEN MAKING WAVES

From fundraising to rescue –
women who have made RNLI history

Imagine a lifeboat rescue from the past and you'll probably think of a crew of bearded men in sou'westers battling the waves in a big wooden boat. And, while all lifeboat volunteers were men during the RNLI's first 150 years, women began to join crews from the late 1960s.

Women such as the fundraisers of Newcastle, County Down played a vital role in keeping the RNLI afloat.

Before that time, however, women weren't allowed to be part of the crews who went out to sea. They were expected to stay at home to look after children and help in other aspects of village life. There were also still a lot of superstitions around the idea of allowing women on boats; for many sailors, including lifeboat crew, the presence of a woman on a ship was thought to anger the sea and be an omen of bad luck.

Although they couldn't be part of the rescue crew, that didn't stop women in coastal communities around the UK and Ireland from playing a crucial role in the lifeboat service, right from the very beginning. Launching the boats was, and still is, a vital part of any rescue mission. And in some communities in the early days of the lifeboat service, it was a job done almost exclusively by women.

Every man to the boat, every woman to the ropes!

Launching the lifeboats was not without its dangers and struggles, especially for the first 'lady launchers' who, just like their male counterparts, would drop everything when the call came in and rush to the lifeboat station to get the rescue started.

The lifeboats back then were heavy wooden vessels, movable only with coarse ropes and brute force. They often needed to be hauled across quite difficult stretches of land and into choppy waters that were unprotected by harbours or modern sea defences. The women launching the boats would have to heave the boats into the water, going in up to their necks, all while wearing their regular clothes – likely to have been long, heavy skirts with petticoats underneath.

The conditions were often treacherous, even at the shoreline, with gale-force winds and pitch-black skies. There were no waterproof jackets, no technical equipment and no powerful searchlights. All they had was each other, the will to succeed and a boatload of courage.

While some stations were able to use horses to launch lifeboats, others relied on people to launch – with a handful of stations dependent on their 'lady launchers'. This was the case for almost 150 years, until the first RNLI tractors arrived and forever transformed lifeboat launching.

A lifeboat crew launched from 1852 to 1946 at Hauxley, Northumberland – it was thanks to women's strength that the lifeboat could reach the surf.

FOCUS ON: DUNGENESS

Dungeness in Kent was the last station to use the traditional manual launch methods, and its 'lady launchers' – as they were known locally – became legendary for their work. Dungeness is an especially difficult place from which to launch a lifeboat; in those days the lifesaving craft had to cross a shingled headland. Before tractors were introduced, the boat had to be pulled with ropes across wooden skids. Positioning the skids in front of the boat as it was pulled towards the water required skill and strength. A wrong placement could mean a damaged boat or, worse, an injured person. Strong easterly winds could affect the boat's course, so considerable precision and good judgement were needed to simply get the boat to the sea.

Once at the shore, the launchers had to wade deep into the water in their clothes to get the boat safely afloat. As a result, the women of RNLI Dungeness were held in high esteem for

The Dungeness 'lady launchers' continued to help pull the lifeboat into the sea right up to the 1950s.

Doris and Ben Tart. From the early 1900s to 1965, much of the Dungeness crew was made up of members of the Tart and Oiller families.

their efforts and have twice, in 1932 and 1974, been accorded the RNLI's prestigious Thanks of the Institution Inscribed on Vellum award. Two female launchers from Dungeness, Madge Tart and her sister-in-law Ellen Tart, from a family whose members helped to crew and launch the Dungeness lifeboat for more than a century, were each awarded the institution's Gold Badge in 1953. And in 1979 Ellen Tart's daughters Doris and Joan Bates were each awarded Gold Badges in recognition of 44 years' and 37 years' service respectively. By then, the Dungeness station had received a launching tractor, bringing the era of 'lady launchers' to an end.

As well as heaving the lifeboat across shingle into the sea, the women of Dungeness faced the tough job of getting it back to station after a rescue.

Female firsts

Grace Darling was the first woman to receive a medal for her bravery from the RNLI. Although not a crew member herself, she was the daughter of a lighthouse keeper. On 7 September 1838 Grace spotted a number of desperate people clinging to Big Harcar rock off the Northumberland coast. They were the survivors of the devastating shipwreck of the SS *Forfarshire*. Grace and her father knew that the local lifeboat, with Grace's brother among the crew, would not reach them in time and so they went to rescue them.

The tide and wind were so strong that they had to row for nearly a mile to avoid the jagged rocks and reach the survivors safely. William leapt out of the boat and onto the rocks, which left Grace to handle the boat alone. To keep it in one place, she had to take both oars and row backwards and forwards, trying to keep it from being smashed on the reef. On the rocks, William found eight men, including one who was badly injured. There was also a woman holding two children, both of whom had died.

The first woman to receive an RNLI Medal for Gallantry was not a lifeboat crew member – Grace Darling rowed her father's boat to the rescue of a shipwrecked crew.

The boat only had room for the injured man and the woman, plus three men, William and Grace. The three men and William rowed together back to the lighthouse. Grace stayed at the lighthouse and looked after the survivors with her mother. Her father and two of the *Forfarshire* crew returned for the other four men.

When news of her selfless, courageous and skilful actions spread, Grace became one of Britain's most celebrated heroes.

In 1969 Elizabeth Hostvedt became the first woman to be a registered crew member in the RNLI. Then 18 years old, she joined Atlantic College's own inshore lifeboat crew, based on the Glamorgan coast. The RNLI's crews were still exclusively male at the time. But in the 1960s the new

Amazed by Grace?
The RNLI's Grace Darling Museum in Bamburgh, Northumberland showcases Grace's upbringing and life in the lighthouse, the events of the rescue that propelled her into the limelight and her status as a national hero. Visit RNLI.org/GraceDarling for more on the museum.

Atlantic College student Elizabeth Hostvedt (pictured here helping pull the lifeboat out to sea) was the RNLI's first female crew member.

LEFT: Frances Glody was the first woman to join an all-weather lifeboat crew.

BELOW LEFT: An all-woman Dun Laoghaire volunteer crew launched their D class to the rescue of four teenagers in 2022. Pictured from left are Hazel Rea, Moselle Hogan and Laura Jackson.

BELOW RIGHT: Sophie Grant-Crookston was the first female lifeguard to receive an RNLI Medal for Gallantry.

inshore lifeboat fleet provided a catalyst for change. Women were accepted to crew these lighter, more manoeuvrable vessels, and they more than proved their capability.

Twelve years later Frances Glody became the first female crew member of an all-weather lifeboat, joining the crew of the Waveney class *St Patrick*, at Dunmore East, Co. Waterford. There were already three women crewing the inshore lifeboat, but Frances joined the all-weather crew when she took over from her father, who was retiring.

Like the gear and want to know more? Read about the kit and gadgets we use to save lives at sea on page 82.

After her skilful boathandling during the rescue of a fisherman, Porthcawl Helm Aileen Jones was the first female RNLI crew member to receive a Medal for Gallantry.

In 2005 Porthcawl Volunteer Lifeboat Helm Aileen Jones was awarded the RNLI Bronze Medal of Gallantry, making her the first woman in 116 years – and the first ever female crew member – to receive an RNLI medal. The medal was awarded in recognition of her part in the rescue of two fishermen.

In 2005 Sophie Grant-Crookston, a lifeguard at Perranporth, Cornwall, became the RNLI's first female lifeguard to receive a medal for Gallantry: she received the Bronze Medal. Sophie, then aged 20, rescued a surfer who'd been sucked into a cave by the tide and was trapped on a ledge, unable to get out.

These days it's not uncommon for all-female crews to launch – crews like Aberdovey volunteers Abi Hinton, Kate Jones, Rhiannon Macefield and Alice Beetlestone (left to right).

Feminine fits

In 2018 the RNLI's all-weather lifeboat crew kit got a complete overhaul. The old kit was bulky, and, since its last redesign, new technical fabrics had emerged that could revolutionise the kit, making it lighter and easier to move in. For the first time female crew members had kit designed with their shape in mind. This included the introduction of female-fit base layers, contoured for a close fit to ensure sweat is wicked away from the skin, keeping the wearer warmer for longer. The new kit also included a shorter leg option, and a new design that meant women no longer had to remove multiple layers of clothing to take a toilet break while out on a long shout.

Dunbar Crew Member Becs Miller pictured wearing the RNLI's new kit that includes sizes and shapes especially for women, supplied by Helly Hansen.

'For the first time, female crew members had kit designed with their shape in mind'

Beyond crew: the women making waves behind the scenes

Today women continue to shape the history of the RNLI in many ways. From the architects designing our stations, to the women spearheading our fundraising, and the designers and engineers innovating at our lifeboat centres in Dorset and the Isle of Wight, women are now at the very heart of the RNLI – and always will be.

Engineering is an especially vital role at the RNLI, and we are working hard to ensure women and girls are integral to our future growth with initiatives like the annual RNLI Women in Engineering event. This event – for girls aged 11 to 13 – is held at the RNLI College in Poole, and aims to inspire them to consider careers in engineering.

In 2024 the RNLI's most senior volunteer is a woman: our Chair, Janet Legrand (Hon) KC. Meanwhile, 200 years since they first dragged the lifeboats to the shore, women are still launching our boats. There are over 80 female launchers – now known, alongside their male colleagues, as shore crew – at lifeboat stations around the UK and Ireland.

At Barmouth in Gwynedd, lifeboat volunteer Glesni Williams has close historical connections with the RNLI. Her three-times grandfather William Griffith served on *The Chieftain* as bowman and second coxswain from 1939 until 1966. Her great-uncle John Stockford served from 1964 until 1992 and was awarded the RNLI's Silver Medal for Gallantry, the first to be awarded to the crew of an inshore lifeboat. In her grandfather's time, female crew members were unheard of – now Glesni is proudly following in her family's lifeboating footsteps.

6
THE KINDNESS OF STRANGERS
How we've been raising funds for 200 years

For many people, it comes as something of a surprise to learn that the RNLI is and always has been a charity. Ever since Sir William Hillary appealed to London's most generous philanthropists to help him fund and launch the organisation, the RNLI has depended on donations and support from the public.

But how do we raise the amounts of money required to provide the kind of 24/7 lifesaving service that we do? And who are the people making sure those funds get to us? There are thousands of volunteers who have given their time and energy to raise those funds. Whether it's an old-fashioned street collection, a sponsored run or the harnessing of more modern technology, we've been finding innovative ways to raise funds for over 200 years.

PREVIOUS PAGE: Tower crew member and RNLI fundraising volunteer Suzanne Goldberg collects at Waterloo train station on London Lifeboat Day for the Mayday appeal.

Money talk
In 1825 the RNLI's first annual report suggested that the charity would need around £3,750 to pay for its 'commitments' in 1826. In 2022 the RNLI's charitable spend was £188M. Most of this was on lifeboat and lifeguard rescue services.

BOTTOM RIGHT: In Lytham St Annes, Lancashire, the community gathers for the dedication of the memorial to the 27 crew members from Southport and St Annes lost in the 1886 *Mexico* disaster.

BOTTOM LEFT: The efforts of Sir Charles Macara (pictured) and his wife Marion, who were so moved by the *Mexico* disaster, heralded a new dawn in RNLI fundraising.

The first street collection

On a Saturday afternoon in 1891 thousands of people flocked to the centre of Manchester to catch a glimpse of something they had never seen before: lifeboat crew members and their lifesaving craft parading through the streets.

The lifeboats were from Lytham St Annes, Lancashire, and Southport, Merseyside, where the crews had, just a few years earlier, been devastated by the loss of 27 crew members during the rescue of a German boat *Mexico*, a tally of lost crew lives that remains the worst in RNLI history. In an attempt to provide for the many families left without husbands and fathers, a local businessman Sir Charles Macara, along with his wife Marion, arranged for the boats to be pulled through the city for everyone to see. Purses and buckets were passed among the enthralled crowds for loose change, and over £5,000 was

'The crews had, just a few years earlier, been devastated by the loss of 27 lifeboatmen' raised on what would come to be known as Lifeboat Saturday. The volunteers and donors that day didn't know it, but this was fundraising history in the making.

Not only was Lifeboat Saturday the first ever known charity street collection, but for the first time the donors weren't wealthy philanthropists, but generous ordinary people. Our volunteers have been collecting loose change for the charity ever since. One hundred and thirty years later, Lifeboat Day is still one of the biggest annual fundraising days in London, with collectors shaking boxes and buckets on the streets and in train stations across the capital. Fundraising branch members in all of the UK and Ireland's major cities manage to collect hundreds of thousands of pounds and euros every year. On the coast, flag days and lifeboat weeks are some of the biggest events in local calendars. And as we move to an increasingly cashless society, volunteers have responded by carrying a different sort of collection box – one with no slots for coins or notes. Donors can now make contactless donations with a quick wave of their debit cards or phones.

One hundred and thirty years on from the first charity street collection, fundraisers joined forces with lifeboat crew members and supporters to recreate the 1891 photograph in Manchester city centre.

FOCUS ON: BOXING CLEVER

There have been many different designs for the collection boxes used by our fundraisers in street collections. Here are just a few from the archive:

1 The oldest collection box in the RNLI's heritage collection dates back to 1860. It's inscribed: 'Charity is kind. For the benefit of the Life Boat Institution.'

2 This brass collecting box, thought to be mid–19th century, shows a picture of a lifeboat pulled by a carriage.

3 Shaped like a lifebuoy, this tin box dates from 1895 and carries the inscription: 'Royal National Life Boat Institution'. Only a thousand of these were ever made.

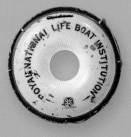

4 The slipway collecting box, first seen in the 1960s, lets you push the lifeboat into the boathouse and then 'launch' it with coins. It's inscribed: 'The life-boats need your help.'

5 Contactless collection box. No cash on you? Just tap to donate.

Sponsored activities
are a crucial source
of income for the RNLI.
Whether you're cycling,
skydiving or undertaking
another outdoor
challenge, you could
help fund lifesaving
kit and training.

From the Ladies Lifeboat Guild to today's fundraising branches

The first Lifeboat Saturday was also the catalyst for what would eventually become one of the most effective fundraising forces in the charity: the Ladies Lifeboat Guild. Seeing the success of the street collection that Lady Marion Macara and her husband Charles had organised, Lady Marion went on to create fundraising committees. She wrote letters to all her well-connected friends to encourage them to support the lifeboats. The idea spread and, 30 years later, at an annual meeting overseen by the Prince of Wales in 1921, RNLI Ladies' Guilds around the country joined forces to become the Ladies Lifeboat Guild. Today, while the spirit and ethos of the original Ladies Lifeboat Guild live on, our fundraising branches are not so gender-specific and everyone is welcome.

RNLI fundraising branches can be found in villages, towns and cities across the UK and Ireland. They arrange collections, organise events and make the best cupcakes around.

Making it personal: the fundraisers who go above and beyond

The RNLI is fortunate to have the support and dedication of many brilliant fundraisers, and every donation, no matter how small, makes a difference. Some of our most amazing fundraisers are not the folk who do things like jumping out of planes and running around entire countries, but those who quietly and modestly hold cake sales, run tombolas and turn up for bucket collections outside their local supermarket in the rain. And behind all of these efforts are all of the associated, less glamorous jobs, like doing risk assessments, sending off forms, cleaning up afterwards and other unseen tasks. Our fundraisers do these things without any desire for acknowledgement or praise, some of them contributing their free time for decades.

Every year runners lace up for the lifesavers, whether they're tackling jaunty jogs or long distances like the London Marathon (pictured).

For many, there is a personal story behind the fundraising. In 2019 12-year-old RNLI fundraiser Keiran Reid from Avoch in Scotland raised over £10,000 for the RNLI with charity car washes, cake sales and fancy-dress events. Keiran was six years old when his father was lost at sea while fishing in the waters around Orkney.

Others take on epic physical challenges such as marathons. In 1978 Rosemary Whitton rode her donkey Sweet William 278 miles from St Ives Lifeboat Station in Cornwall to Hyde Park Corner in London. The pair made it to the capital in 28 days. Rosemary raised over £1,500 and wrote afterwards, 'I proved to myself that a journey of this sort can still be undertaken if proper training, preparation and planning is carried out, and the RNLI has tremendous support throughout the country, even in places remote from the sea.'

More recently, Alex Ellis-Roswell made an incredible journey on foot around the Irish and UK coastline (with no donkey support team to lighten his load!). Alex set off from Minnis Bay in Kent in 2014 and finished his walk back where he started on 11 November 2017, greeted by local and national supporters, the press, RNLI and his mother. Alex said the biggest lesson he learned was: 'People are good. Trust people, help people.'

Alex Ellis-Roswell walked the whole of the Irish and UK coastline in aid of the RNLI.

'The RNLI is fortunate to have the support and dedication of many brilliant fundraisers, and every donation, no matter how small, makes a difference'

The RNLI has its own
face-to-face fundraising
team. They head to events
and beaches in the summer
to provide safety advice
and offer visitors the chance
to become a regular donor
to the RNLI.

Leaving a gift in your Will

Many people choose to leave a legacy gift to the RNLI in their Will. Supporters who name the RNLI in their will often feel a real connection to the RNLI and its history, and to the crew's presence in the places they've loved. Leaving a legacy gift is a way to be there for our crew, protecting them, providing equipment and skills, for generations to come. No matter how large or small the legacy gift, supporters can have their name added to the side of a lifeboat, making them part of the RNLI family for years to come.

Retail therapy

The RNLI sells its own souvenirs, gifts, clothes and much more – online and at shops usually found next to lifeboat stations around the coast (thanks to the volunteers who run them). Every pound and euro of profit helps save more lives, so have a browse at shop.RNLI.org or find shops to visit at RNLI.org/shops.

Every gift, large or small, helps save lives. One supporter left his Ferraris to the RNLI.

Fundraising for the future

As well as accepting pounds and euros, the RNLI has long benefited from those donating their unwanted foreign coins. But in 2014 donors' wallets went digital when we became the first major UK charity to accept the cryptocurrency Bitcoin. Other supporters have left treasured possessions in their legacies to help raise funds in their memory. Gifts that didn't quite fit into the collecting tin have included bottles of brandy, antique swords and two Ferraris.

Whatever the donation and however it comes to us, we'll keep on working with our generous supporters to raise funds and save lives at sea for another 200 years.

The RNLI's shops can be found all around the coast, plus you can order online at shop. RNLI.org. Every pound and euro you spend helps save lives at sea.

7

GEAR AND GADGETS

The evolution of lifesaving RNLI kit and technology

One thing that hasn't changed that much in 200 years of our lifesaving history is how the weather, and plenty of it, tends to play a major part in many of the rescues our crew members launch to. Be it driving rain and gale-force winds or blazing sunshine and uncomfortably high temperatures, our volunteers often find themselves battling the elements while also being called upon to rescue others in difficulty.

To protect themselves and to help them do their job as safely as possible – as well as keeping themselves safe and dry during training exercises – our crews have always needed specialised clothing. From the very first oilskins and cork lifejackets to today's breathable all-weather gear, we've continually pushed the limits of modern technology in the name of saving lives and coming home safely.

Headgear

Before the invention of protective hooded jackets, staying warm and dry while going to sea in open, oar-powered rowing boats was a tough call. To keep their heads warm, RNLI crews wore bright red woollen caps either on their own or under black sou'wester hats. The sou'westers were water-proofed with oil and had a long back flap to protect the neck from spray. This type of headgear was the standard for over a century. In the 1930s a band of volunteers knitted over 1,500 hybrid 'scarf-helmets' to keep crew members' necks warm, but this design didn't catch on.

Today's lifeboat crew helmets provide better protection than ever.

The standard kit for lifeboat crew from the 1960s to the 1980s included the 'bump cap', designed to protect volunteers using increasingly faster lifeboats. The crew kit also included the Beaufort lifejacket.

'Staying warm and dry while going to sea in open boats was a tough call'

By the 1960s the introduction of the faster Waveney class lifeboat gave an increasingly bumpy ride for volunteer lifeboat crew, so there was a move towards more hard-wearing headgear for increased protection at high speeds. In the 1970s, the introduction of the Atlantic 21 inshore lifeboat meant that crew members, exposed to the elements in these smaller, faster lifeboats, needed even more protection from the spray. A visor was press-studded onto a motorcycle helmet from the manufacturer, allowing volunteers to race to a rescue without the horizontal hail of sea spray hitting their eyes at high speeds.

By the 1990s, with faster lifeboats and improved communication technology transforming the way rescues were performed, a project was set up to explore integrating these two developments – a helmet that could provide protection while also allowing crew members to communicate effectively with each other at sea, with the crew on land and with other rescue services. A number of helmets from different fields of activity and different manufacturers were tested – tank-crew helmets, equestrian, canoeing and motorcycle helmets – some with their own cordless intercoms. After a week of pilot trials with five coxswains and a training vessel, in 1995 a lightweight, close-fitting, easy-to-clean, easy-to-hear-through, strong 'skull cap'-type helmet was given the go-ahead.

Today's helmets take 1990s technology even further: sleek, lightweight, robust, visored headpieces with the facility to add torches, cameras and comms equipment, all specifically modified to work best for the lifeboat and the crew who are using it.

Lifeboat crew members from Abersoch, Gwynedd, wearing their cork lifejackets in the late 1800s.

Lifejackets

Until the first motorised lifeboat came along in 1905, our volunteers had to manually row or sail their lifeboats to rescues in stormy seas. So when the idea of creating a lifejacket was first mooted, its most basic requirement – beyond being buoyant – was that it should be flexible enough to move comfortably with crew members as they rowed.

In 1854 a range of materials for the new lifejacket were put through rigorous testing for buoyancy, weight, durability and water resistance. If a component didn't meet the RNLI's standards for enduring the lifesaving task at hand, the material was immediately discarded. Some of the unsuccessful designs included an inflatable canvas jacket with large pockets of air – this failed because it punctured too easily. Horsehair and rushes were also considered, but although the materials were light and buoyant, neither were waterproof or durable enough for lifejackets. Bark from trees such as the baobab and balsa were also sufficiently light and buoyant, but both were hard to obtain and very expensive to buy.

The winning lifeboat jacket design was created by an RNLI inspector, Captain Ward. He used narrow strips of common, circular cork, which were fitted together and sewn into a canvas vest. This was the first lifejacket ever to be issued to lifeboat crew members, and although it was bulky, it floated well (holding a buoyancy of 25lb each), was hard-wearing and a resounding success with crew members. The lifejackets were created in two different sizes to fit the builds of the lifeboat crew. They were also made large enough to be passed over a casualty's head and shoulders.

BELOW: Whitby lifeboat Crew Member Henry Freeman was the sole survivor of a lifeboat disaster off the Yorkshire coast in 1861.

BELOW RIGHT: Ballycotton lifeboat Coxswain Patrick Sliney, pictured wearing a kapok lifejacket in 1936 after receiving a Gold Medal for Gallantry.

Modern RNLI crew lifejackets allow for a greater degree of movement than their cork and kapok predecessors.

The lifesaving efficiency of the cork lifejackets was soon demonstrated in a tragic rescue attempt off the Yorkshire coast in 1861. A huge storm wrecked 200 boats on the east coast, with the Whitby lifeboat crew launching five times to rescue survivors from the ships. But on the sixth launch, tragedy struck. A freak wave hit the lifeboat and capsized it, with all but one of the lifeboat crew lost. The sole survivor of this tragedy was Henry Freeman, who remained alive for one simple reason: he was the only crew member who had been wearing a cork lifejacket.

In the 1900s, kapok, a fibre of the silk-cotton tree, replaced cork as the major buoyancy component in our lifejackets. Kapok is three times more buoyant than cork and doesn't absorb water. The first kapok lifejackets were bulky and uncomfortable, but our designers refined the jackets until crews were happy leaving their cork lifejackets behind. The kapok lifejacket became one of the RNLI's most enduring innovations, with crews using this lifejacket for almost 70 years.

By the 1970s innovations in plastics and other materials meant the use of foam in a lifejacket could significantly increase its buoyancy, enabling a crew member to also support the person being rescued. These new Beaufort lifejackets ensured that volunteers would float face-up in the water, even if they were unconscious. The lifejacket got a new bright orange colour as well, making it more visible in the water than previous jackets.

'Today's inshore and all-weather lifejackets feature lights, flare pockets, spray hoods, whistles and safety lines'

As lifeboat design became more and more attuned to varied locations, with the needs of individual crews around the UK and Ireland changing in tandem, the design of the lifejackets they wore evolved too. We began to see separate lifejackets being used for different disciplines. The bulkier gear of all-weather lifeboat crews meant they needed a more compact lifejacket that inflated automatically via a built-in gas canister on hitting the water. Inshore crews, who entered the water much more frequently, got a bigger lifejacket with built-in buoyancy.

Today's inshore and all-weather lifejackets feature lights, flare pockets, spray hoods, whistles and safety lines, while offering our volunteers unrestricted movement onboard and in the water. Once inflated, these modern lifejackets keep the wearer's head clear of the water.

Lifeboat crew kit has changed beyond recognition over the years – from the oilskins and cork lifejackets of yesteryear to today's waterproof, breathable gear, well-equipped helmets and inflatable lifejackets.

Protection from the elements

Staying warm and dry has always been the most important function of a lifeboat volunteer's kit. In the RNLI's early days, that meant crews would wear woollen fisherman's ganseys and blue woollen trousers. Wool, when knitted tightly, gave protection from the cold and acted as a water repellent. Later jumpers had 'RNLI' or the crew position (for example, 'Coxswain') knitted into the chest. But in 1854 our crews moved to waterproof oilskins, which would be a mainstay in many different forms for over a century. Initially black, these changed in 1904 to our signature bright yellow for higher visibility. The long yellow coat also had 'RNLI' printed on the sleeve, enabling people to identify their rescuers at a glance.

But by the 1970s yellow made way for orange. While oilskins kept water out, they also kept condensation in, giving the bodies inside no chance to breathe. With overlapping trousers and jacket, the new orange foul-weather gear was roomier, allowing air to circulate as our volunteers went about their business onboard the lifeboat. The 1970s also saw the introduction of the first RNLI one-piece drysuit. Made from rubber, it was designed to be slipped on quickly by inshore lifeboat crews before they set off and meant they could move about much more freely.

Upcycled kit

What becomes of older kit when an updated model or a new design is introduced? When they reach the end of their service lives, RNLI lifejackets are decommissioned. But to save them from going to landfill, they were upcycled into a hard-wearing and water-resistant product range. Bags, wallets and pouches made from decommissioned lifejackets have all been on sale in our shops over the years. And with every sale, the money comes back to the RNLI to keep even more people safe.

Yellow is the colour

Lifeboat crew members, such as these all-weather and inshore crews at Fleetwood, Lancashire, are well protected by their modern kit.

After a decade of orange all-weather gear, we switched back to yellow in the 1980s, this time in a new, brighter and easier-to-spot shade. The new kits were lighter, with better ventilation, courtesy of early breathable materials, and they made movement freer than ever for all-weather lifeboat crews. Technical fabrics and designs continued to be honed, and in the 1990s we added several new features: large, smartphone-friendly pockets that meant coxswains could take calls directly from the coastguard, and reinforced hems and replaceable straps to ensure that salopettes were more robust and lasted longer.

'The new kits were lighter, with better ventilation, and they made movement freer'

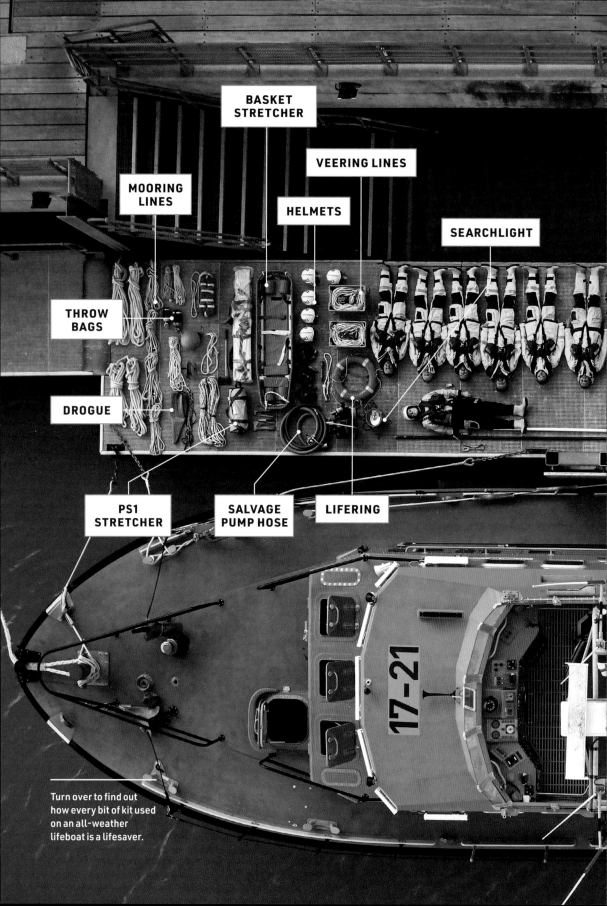

BASKET STRETCHER

VEERING LINES

MOORING LINES

HELMETS

SEARCHLIGHT

THROW BAGS

DROGUE

PS1 STRETCHER

SALVAGE PUMP HOSE

LIFERING

17-21

Turn over to find out how every bit of kit used on an all-weather lifeboat is a lifesaver.

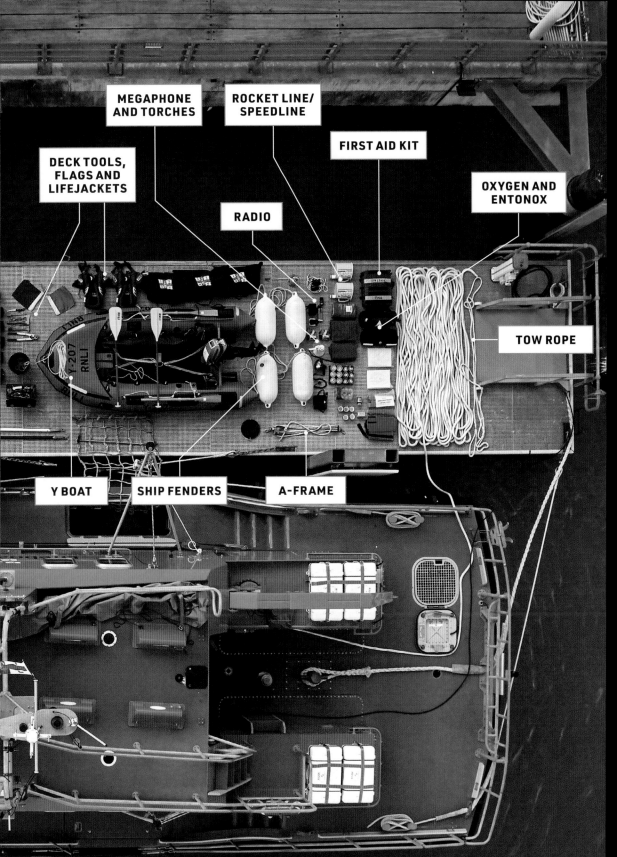

MEGAPHONE AND TORCHES

ROCKET LINE/ SPEEDLINE

FIRST AID KIT

DECK TOOLS, FLAGS AND LIFEJACKETS

OXYGEN AND ENTONOX

RADIO

TOW ROPE

Y BOAT

SHIP FENDERS

A-FRAME

What gear is used aboard modern lifeboats?

Tow rope
200m long, made of polyester for strength

Torches
To light the way aboard boats and along the coast

Oxygen and Entonox
For emergency first aid. Entonox – also known as 'gas and air' – is used for pain relief

Radio
A hand-held VHF radio for crew transferring ashore or to casualty vessels

First aid kit
Everything needed for emergency first aid – including bandages, gauzes and collars

Ship fenders
To protect the lifeboat when alongside a casualty vessel

Rocket line/speedline
A pyrotechnic used to pass lines to casualty vessels – 275m of 4mm floating line

Y boat
A small inflatable daughter boat, for getting in close to rocks through shallow water

A-frame
Used to lift or lower casualties over the side of the lifeboat, with a safe working load of 200kg

Deck tools
For emergency repairs, or for freeing casualties when trapped

Megaphone
For when the crew need to be heard over the roar of engines or waves

Flags
To aid communication with a nearby rescue helicopter – green for 'continue', red for 'cease operations immediately'

Searchlight
A very bright mountable light with optical reflector to direct the light

Lifering
Passed to casualties in the water to help keep them afloat until they can be brought onboard

Salvage pump hose
Used to remove water from a flooded casualty vessel, powered by a petrol or diesel engine

Veering lines
Used with an anchor to keep the bow facing to sea for quick escape near cliffs and rocks. Made of polypropylene to float and stay visible

Basket stretcher
To make evacuating casualties easier, can also be used with the A-frame to bring a casualty onboard

PS1 stretcher
A flexible stretcher used to extract a casualty from a confined space or drag them across rough ground – can be placed in the basket stretcher for lifting

Drogue
Used in heavy weather to slow a casualty vessel and help maintain directional stability if the vessel has steering problems

Throw bags
Used in open water and swift-water environments to bring a casualty closer for rescuing

Mooring lines
To tie a vessel afloat, alongside a pontoon, jetty, wall or mooring buoy. Made of polyester for its stretch capabilities

Fishing barometers

While not an RNLI invention, the decision to use aneroid barometers widely in lifeboat stations and subsequently on individual fishing vessels dramatically reduced the number of deaths within fishing communities in the late Victorian period. These simple devices can detect changes in air pressure, which can indicate an impending change in weather conditions and therefore provide a warning for small vessels that might otherwise be caught out by storms. An article in the *Lifeboat* journal of 1882, reporting the decision to provide barometers to fishing boats, stated:

At present it is notorious that the masters of our small fishing craft hardly ever think of carrying with them an aneroid, and thus, when in mid-ocean, they are without the most hopeful means of forecasting the disasters which too often overtake them when gales of wind suddenly spring up.

By means of those barometers and their timely warnings, it is certain that the NATIONAL LIFE-BOAT INSTITUTION must have indirectly contributed to the saving of the lives of a large number of fishermen. It will thus be seen what beneficial results are likely to accrue to life and property if this fresh important step of the Institution is appreciated and encouraged by the owners of fishing vessels.

As well as supplying aneroid barometers to fishing crews, the RNLI also provided some communities with one. In St Davids, embrokeshire, former Coxswain Malcolm Gray MBE is pictured next to the tiny city's barometer. Mariners were able to check it before going to sea, long before accurate weather forecasts were available.

'The decision to use barometers ... dramatically reduced the number of deaths'

8

SAFER ALL ROUND

*How the RNLI saves lives by
sharing skills and advice*

The incidents that lead to calls for help in the water are often avoidable – and many of the rescues that the RNLI carries out can be difficult and dangerous. So how is the charity helping people to stay safe through prevention?

Safety through prevention

When it comes to saving lives at sea, prevention is better than cure. The RNLI will always provide rescue services to cover times when things go wrong in the water, but our safety volunteers and campaigns have prevented countless tragedies from ever occurring through their ongoing safety advice. This helps people to avoid getting into danger in the first place, as well as giving them a greater chance of surviving if they do find themselves in difficulty.

It's not a new approach – RNLI founder Sir William Hillary's Tower of Refuge, built on a reef in Douglas Bay, provided a sanctuary for shipwrecked sailors to keep them safe until they could get help (see Chapter 1), and later in the 19th century the RNLI provided aneroid barometers that warned fishing crews of dangerous weather (see page 98).

Water safety has grown to become a fundamental part of the RNLI's lifesaving activities in the 21st century. Lifeguards spend much of their time offering advice and spotting hazards on the beach before the worst happens. Our education work with schools and youth groups gives children advice that one day could prevent them from drowning. Campaigns and partnerships share safety messages far and wide. And much of the RNLI's international work is focused on interventions that provide skills and knowledge to ensure people can keep themselves safer, rather than rely on being rescued.

Initially, much of the charity's safety work was centred on traditional sea users such as commercial fishing crews and recreational sailors. That has now widened to encompass all sorts of other coastal leisure activities, from offering open-water-swimming safety tips to encouraging sea anglers and paddleboarders to wear lifejackets and buoyancy aids.

PREVIOUS PAGE: The RNLI have partnered with The Black Swimming Association (BSA). The pictured safety training event with the BSA included throwbag training, which shows people how to use the public water-safety equipment available next to waterways.

A shocking statistic

RNLI research has shown that around 50% of those who drown every year never intended to go into the water in the first place. Many slipped, tripped or fell in. Others were trapped by rising tides, swept into the sea by waves or went to rescue someone. That's one of the reasons why the charity has worked closely with Professor Mike Tipton MBE at the Extreme Environments Laboratory at the University of Portsmouth, and RNLI council member. His pioneering research into the effects of cold-water shock found that it's one of the biggest stresses our bodies can face and can occur in water temperatures of under 15°C. Even on the relatively warm south coast of England, sea temperatures don't tend to rise above 15°C until July, and in many parts of Scotland and Northern Ireland they usually stay under 15°C throughout the year. The sudden cooling of the skin by cold water reduces skin blood flow and increases your heart rate and blood pressure. It also causes an involuntary gasp for breath, and breathing rates can change uncontrollably, sometimes increasing as much as tenfold. Both of these responses can provoke an immediate sense of panic, increasing the chance of inhaling water directly into the lungs.

Float to Live
As well as encouraging people to stay safe when next to water, the RNLI's biggest-ever safety campaign provides a skill to use if you do fall in: Float to Live. More than 30 people have approached the RNLI to say that they used this skill to help save their own life.

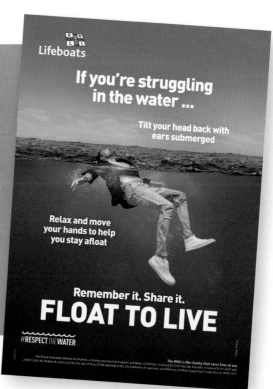

Partnerships for prevention

The RNLI helps prevent tragedies by partnering with and working along-side other organisations, including the Maritime and Coastguard Agency, the National Water Safety Forum, and the Black Swimming Association (BSA). The BSA is dedicated to ensuring that people of African, Caribbean and Asian heritage have equal and equitable access to aquatics, as well as being able to enjoy a safe experience in and around the water. It was founded by elite swimmer Alice Dearing, journalist Seren Jones, producer and creator Ed Accura and business consultant Danielle Obe.

Black Swimming Association (BSA) Chair Danielle Obe at a joint BSA and RNLI safety session at the RNLI College.

Lifeboat crew members on the pitch during the All-Ireland Senior Hurling semi-final at Croke Park.

The Gaelic Athletic Association (GAA) is Ireland's largest sporting organisation. It promotes Gaelic games such as Hurling, Football, Handball and Rounders. It also promotes Irish music, song and dance and the Irish language. The RNLI has formed a special partnership with the GAA in a team effort to educate communities on how to stay safe in and around the water. The partnership is part of the GAA Healthy Clubs' programme and has seen volunteer lifeboat crews visiting GAA clubs to give water safety talks. Lifeboat crew members from around the island of Ireland were invited onto the pitch during the All-Ireland Senior Hurling semi-final at Croke Park in Dublin to promote the partnership with the GAA.

Useless unless worn

As well as pioneering the use of lifejackets among its
own crews, the RNLI has played a key role in encouraging
those who go afloat to use lifejackets and buoyancy
aids. Work with commercial fishing crews has included
sessions in the RNLI's dedicated sea-survival pool.
Fishermen were invited to experience what it feels like
to fall into the water in their full kit without a lifejacket.
Their heavy gear weighed them down and they struggled
to stay afloat without assistance. When they then jumped
into the pool wearing a lifejacket, the benefits of staying
afloat with their face out of the water led them to
champion the use of lifejackets among their fishing
communities. Similar sessions with recreational sea
anglers also had successful outcomes.

'The benefits of staying afloat with their face out of the water led [fishermen] to champion the use of lifejackets'

A good call

We urge anyone taking to the water to carry a means of calling for help in a waterproof pouch – something our crews have seen save many lives. Call 999 or 112 and ask for the coastguard in a coastal/sea emergency.

...urage, nothing is impossible

Sir William Hillary, Founder of the RNLI

SELFLESS SACRIFICE

In the RNLI's history, many crew members never returned after launching to the rescue

The dangerous and selfless nature of lifesaving means that in our 200-year history a number of our brave crew members have lost their lives in the name of saving others. When lifeboat crew members are lost, communities, as well as families, are devastated. These heroes are always remembered proudly in their local lifeboat communities, often with memorials and statues. And the RNLI Memorial Sculpture in Poole, Dorset, names each and every one of them.

The memorial was unveiled in 2009, and it serves as a source of inspiration for current and future generations of lifeboat crew, lifeguards, supporters and fundraisers. It reminds us that there are still people who volunteer to carry out selfless acts of heroism to help others; we will always remember their sacrifice. There are 778 names from every corner of the UK and Ireland, representing RNLI crew members and other courageous lifesavers from the early 1800s onwards who did not return after they answered the call to save lives at sea. Each has their own story, and in many cases those listed saved the lives of others before losing their own.

The sculpture, by artist Sam Holland, depicts a person in a boat reaching out to save someone else. The large metallic plinth leans at an improbable angle, hinting at the force of the wind and the waves, while the two figures seem to strain every sinew to survive. Passers-by cannot fail to be awestruck by the sculpture – including the lifeboat crew and lifeguards arriving for training at the RNLI College. Above the list of names of those who sacrificed their own lives to save others, the sculpture bears the motto of RNLI founder Sir William Hillary: 'With courage, nothing is impossible.'

Never forgotten

The RNLI's courageous history features many tales of tragedy, from the loss of 15 crew in Dun Laoghaire on Christmas Eve in 1895 and the 17 crew from Rye Harbour lost on a shout in 1928 to the five crew members lost at Fraserburgh in 1970, and the many more volunteers who have died while trying to help others. Radio, engines, improved kit and innovations in safety have meant that our crews are safer than ever. But they will never underestimate the power and dangers of the sea.

The names of all those listed on the RNLI memorial are listed at the back of this book.

Remembering Penlee

The Penlee lifeboat disaster is the last time a whole crew was lost.

On 19 December 1981, the Falmouth Coastguard received a call from the *Union Star*, a coaster making its way from Holland to Ireland with a cargo of agricultural fertiliser. The ship's engines had failed and would not restart. There was a fierce storm under way, and the rough seas and powerful winds were blowing the vessel towards the treacherous Cornish coastline. There were eight people onboard; as well as the captain and his crew of four, the captain's wife and two teenage stepdaughters were with them, having joined the ship so that they could be together for the holidays.

In Mousehole, word spread that the lifeboat might be needed and Penlee's *Solomon Browne* was put on standby. A dozen men answered the call for crew, but only eight were required. A rescue under such severe conditions would be difficult and Coxswain William Trevelyan Richards chose the best crew for the task.

ABOVE: Penlee's *Solomon Browne* lifeboat and crew saved many lives before the tragic night of 19 December 1981.

RIGHT: The Penlee page of the RNLI memorial book, marking the names of the crew who were lost in the service to the *Union Star*.

'There was a fierce storm underway, rough seas and powerful winds'

PENLEE

19·XII·1981

William Trevelyan Richards
James Stephen Madron
Nigel Brockman
John Robert Blewett
Charles Thomas Greenhaugh
Kevin Smith
Barrie Robertson Torrie
Gary Lee Wallis

Service to the coaster 'Union Star'

This painting by Tim Thompson depicts the Penlee lifeboat trying to get alongside the *Union Star* in towering seas.

After attempts by an RNAS Sea King helicopter to reach the crew of the *Union Star* failed, the *Solomon Browne* was launched. The helicopter stood by as the wooden 14m Watson class lifeboat launched in hurricane Force 12 winds and 18m waves. The powerless *Union Star* had already lost one anchor, but was desperately trying to hold her position as the lifeboat fought the harsh breaking seas to come alongside.

From the helicopter, lifeboat crew could be seen standing against the railings, throwing lines across to the coaster. Dark shadows of people in fluorescent orange lifejackets were seen to run across the deck from the wheelhouse to the lifeboat, where the crew were waiting to catch them as they jumped. The *Solomon Browne* radioed back to the coastguard – 'We've got four off' – and the helicopter turned back to base, assuming the lifeboat would head to shore.

But the lifeboat decided to make a final rescue attempt – and after that point, all radio contact was lost. The coastguard radioed back to the lifeboat, but there was no response. Ten minutes later, the lights of the *Solomon Browne* disappeared. The helicopter refuelled and took off again. Lifeboats from Sennen Cove, the Lizard and St Mary's also went to help their colleagues, but their searches were unsuccessful. At daybreak, the *Union Star* was found capsized on the rocks by Tater Du Lighthouse and wreck debris from the lifeboat began to wash ashore. There were no survivors from the lifeboat or the *Union Star*.

The lost lifeboat crew members were posthumously awarded gallantry medals, which were presented to their widows and parents by HRH Princess Alice, Duchess of Gloucester, at the Royal Festival Hall, London, on 11 May 1982.

Janet Madron with a photo of her husband James, known as Stephen.

'I'm forever proud of what he did, and what he tried to do,' said Janet Madron BEM, whose husband James – known as Stephen – was lost that night. Janet has fundraised and volunteered at the Penlee RNLI shop ever since. 'After he was lost, I didn't quite know what to do. But I carried on, and I'm so glad that I did because it's such a big part of my life now and I just really enjoy it. I love the whole thing, working in the shop, meeting people, talking to people – it's filled my life up, really.'

Janet received the British Empire Medal (BEM) for her services to the RNLI and, in 2022, was invited to represent the RNLI at the funeral of the charity's longest-serving Patron, Queen Elizabeth II. It was in recognition of Janet's dedication to rebuilding the lifesaving community in Penlee, raising essential funds and inspiring a future generation of lifesavers. 'I wore Stephen's medal and my BEM to the funeral,' said Janet. 'I just felt so proud and so privileged to be a part of it all and represent the RNLI – it was wonderful.'

10

YOUNG LIFESAVERS
How we inspire children and young people

By courtesy of]

LIFE-BOAT ESSAY COMPETITION.

[L.N.A.

Colonel, the Master, of Sempill presenting the Challenge Shields for Greater London and the South East of England. On the Master of Sempill's left is the Mayor of Westminster

With their distinctive yellow crew kit, high-tech craft and feats of incredible bravery in the face of danger, our lifeboat crew members, like all superheroes, have always captured the imagination of children and young people.

Harnessing this enthusiasm to inspire young people to stay safe in and around the water has long been at the heart of our mission. Prevention is better than cure, so it makes sense to help children not only to learn to swim but to respect the water, as well as empowering them with the skills and knowledge of what to do if they find themselves in danger. Much like our lifeboats and the kit we use, the way we reach our young audiences has evolved alongside developing technology and changing lifestyles.

'The average crew member was described as an old bunch of bone and muscle'

Red noses and red faces

In the early 1900s, the RNLI inaugurated an annual essay competition that invited primary school children to write about themes set by the charity. In 1928 the challenge for children was to describe the kind of person that a good crew member should be. Almost 2,000 schools took part, and the highlights were published in the *Lifeboat* journal.

One child wrote that a crew member must be 'perfect, both mentally and physically, and also have the dexterity of an athlete'. Another stated that the crew member 'must be very heavy and healthy to keep their place in the boat'. The average crew member was described as 'an old bunch of bone and muscle', while another child assured readers that they are usually 'very fat'.

Other stipulations for the character of lifeboat crew included that they should always know the front of the boat from the back, as well as being very tall and having the courage of a lion. Good teeth were also important, as toothache would naturally be a hindrance at sea. All lifeboat crew should have red faces and red noses, because they get the very best fresh air. But the child that perhaps summed it up best wrote simply that a lifeboat crew member should 'possess great courage, a spirit of self-sacrifice and a waterproof hat'.

The essay competition clearly touched the imagination of many thousands of children across the UK and Ireland as it ran well into the late 1930s.

A special relationship: *Blue Peter* and the RNLI

In 1966 the children's television programme *Blue Peter* launched an appeal aimed at funding three new D class inflatable lifeboats for the RNLI fleet. Eager young viewers immediately got behind the idea, donating their old paperback books to be sold, and the appeal was so successful that it smashed its original target and funded four inshore craft. Thus began a long friendship between the iconic show and the RNLI.

In 1968 the *Blue Peter* annual featured a special story by Michael Bond in which Paddington Bear finds himself rescued by a lifeboat. And in 1970 two crew members – Roy Cole and Jenny Pelham – appeared on the programme to talk about how the D class was helping the flood rescue effort in East Pakistan. In 1972 a further fundraising appeal enabled the lifeboats at North Berwick and St Agnes to be replaced, and Littlehampton and Beaumaris were given larger Atlantic 21 rigid inflatable lifeboats. Another appeal during 1993 and 1994 was so successful that six inshore lifeboats were replaced, including those at Cleethorpes and Portaferry, and the first *Blue Peter* all-weather lifeboat, a Trent class, was stationed at Fishguard.

North Berwick's D class D-112 lifeboat was named *Blue Peter* – it was funded in 1966 thanks to one of many *Blue Peter* appeals in aid of the RNLI. Presenter Valerie Singleton is pictured onboard.

'Blue Peter viewers funded 28 lifeboats across seven stations'

Over the years, *Blue Peter* viewers have funded 28 lifeboats across seven stations – all named *Blue Peter*. Four of their crews have been honoured with RNLI Medals for Gallantry, including St Agnes Helm Peter David Bliss, who was awarded a Silver Medal for the rescue of an injured surf lifesaver trapped at the base of cliffs. In 2017, celebrating the show's 60th anniversary and the 50 years that had passed since the first *Blue Peter* lifeboat joined the fleet, presenter Lindsey Russell donned the yellow crew kit and went to sea with Beaumaris volunteers. She later tweeted: 'RNLI crews are actual superheroes.'

Storm Force

Paging all future crew! Part of our mission to keep everyone safe in and around the water means getting our message out and creating enthusiasm for water safety among our youngest water users. One way we do this is with Storm Force – our very own club for young people, which reached its 40th year in 2024. Children who join this special crew receive an exciting membership pack, which includes an exclusive crew bag, pencil case, stickers and more. They also receive four issues of *Storm Force* magazine – packed with real rescue stories, comics, games, things to make and do, water safety tips and competitions. They also get access to our online Crew Room, with activities, thrilling rescue videos and other awesome extras.

A year's subscription to *Storm Force* is less than the price of a regular video game, and is a fun and educational gift that lasts. It would make an ideal birthday or Christmas present for the mini crew members in your life.

Ciara has been a huge RNLI fan since her Granny Max signed her up to *Storm Force* a few years ago. She loves spending her pocket money in the Portrush RNLI shop – and we love this brilliant lifeboat she made!

Swim Safe

We know we can help reduce the number of incidents around our coasts and at inland locations by educating children about water safety from a young age. Our Swim Safe programme, in partnership with Swim England, takes our messages and knowledge direct to the people who need it, at beaches and on rivers and lakes around the UK and Ireland. These free, 45-minute Swim Safe sessions for children aged between 7 and 14 help build confidence in and around the water, while teaching vital skills that could save their lives. More than 170,000 young people have taken part at more than 100 locations throughout the UK.

Swim Safe provides free aquatic safety sessions for children aged 7 to 14. For more information, visit swimsafe.org.uk.

Float to Live saves lives

In 2022 a schoolboy from the UK West Midlands saved another boy from drowning thanks to the Float to Live technique he'd read about in his *Storm Force* magazine. Finley Hassall, who was then aged 11 and on holiday in Cornwall, knew exactly what to do when he saw a young boy in trouble in the sea.

Finley saw the boy splashing and struggling, with the waves going over his head. He remembered the article he'd read about Float to Live and told the boy to swim on his back in a starfish shape to regain control of his breathing, helping him to stay calm until an RNLI lifeguard, Guy Potter, arrived to help. The RNLI awarded Finley with a Certificate of Thanks.

Lifeguard Guy Potter presents Finley with a Certificate of Thanks from the RNLI.

**Floating is a life skill that
the RNLI aims to share with
all children and young people**

FOCUS ON: KEEPING YOUNG PEOPLE SAFE ON THE COAST

Around 35 million people visit the coast every summer, and families with young children are among those who need our help the most. If you're taking youngsters to the seaside, make sure they have fun and stay safe by choosing a lifeguarded beach and helping them to learn these simple water safety tips:

Stop and think.
When you're by the water ask yourself: 'Is this a safe place to swim?' and 'Is there a lifeguard nearby?'

Stay together.
Always go to the sea with family or friends. And tell someone where you're going.

Float.
If you get into trouble in the water, try not to panic. Float on your back and stretch out your arms and legs, like you're a big starfish. When you feel calm, put a hand in the air and shout for help.

Call 999 or 112.
If you see someone else in trouble, don't go in the water to help – call 999 or 112.

Get gaming with the RNLI!

Storm Force Rescue is a free-to-download RNLI video game that children can play on phones and tablets. Players can answer the call for help aboard all sorts of lifesaving craft, from lifeguard rescue boards to a Shannon class lifeboat. Search RNLI on the Google Play Store (for Android) or the Apple App Store to download and get rescuing! For more details, see RNLI.org/StormForceRescue.

Inspiring the next generation

What do the different lifeguard flags mean? What should you do if you're caught in a rip current? How do you survive in cold water? Children can learn all this and more through our resources and presentations for schools – all provided thanks to RNLI water safety volunteers.

We provide a range of materials to teachers and tutors to help them bring themes of water safety and lifesaving to their classroom. And for school leavers, the RNLI provides volunteering and employment opportunities that can provide a meaningful career path – from engineering to marketing.

Read more about our Women in Engineering programme on page 67.

Young fundraisers

As well as taking our water safety messages to schools and youth groups, we provide support and inspiration for children of all ages who wish to help raise funds for the RNLI. Many children are inspired to help us raise money either by a school visit from a local lifeboat crew, or from chatting with lifeguards they've met on the beach in the holidays. For others, the inspiration is personal – a family member who has been rescued or a loved one who is part of a crew. Whatever their motivations, our young fundraisers never fail to amaze with their ingenuity, hard work and commitment to raising money for the RNLI's volunteer crews.

Henry James, who raised £1,200 with a sponsored cycle ride from Blackpool lifeboat station to Fleetwood lifeboat station after talking to his neighbour who is a crew member.

11

WARTIME COURAGE

Saving lives in times of turmoil

While stories of wartime often tell of soldiers in combat or of political manoeuvring, there is another story that is not always told: that of the lifeboat volunteers who during both the First and Second World War saved thousands of lives.

As men of fighting age from coastal communities were sent to Europe for combat, it was their fathers and grandfathers, uncles and great-uncles who remained at home to crew the lifeboats. During both wars, the average age of an RNLI volunteer crew member rose to above 55 years, as the older generation kept the lifeboats going on the shores of the home front. Both wars also created very different kinds of rescues for these aging crews. Passenger ships hit by U-boats, downed fighter planes and casualties from Europe were now likely to need their help, as well as local fishing boats or sailing ships caught in bad weather.

First World War

Lifesaving was truly a gruelling task for the RNLI crews of the First World War. Motorised lifeboats were still rare, so most RNLI lifesaving craft were powered by oars, wind and human strength. Things were no less challenging for those who launched the boats, often by hand or with the help of horses, across exposed beaches in high winds, darkness and rain.

The *Lifeboat* journal of December 1939 shared photographs of wartime courage. 'It is on the east and south-east coasts that the burden has been heaviest. From Aldeburgh in Suffolk on 10th September, 1939, the first life-boat was launched to the help of a ship in distress through the war, the Newcastle steamer *Magdapur*, with a crew of 80, sunk by enemy action. The Aldeburgh life-boat rescued 74 men from her. From that day onwards hardly a day has passed without life-boats going out to the rescue somewhere round our coasts.'

RNLI – TO SAVE EVERY ONE

Trusty steeds. Read more about horses and how they've helped us launch the lifeboats on page 173.

Falmouth lifeboat volunteers were among those who risked their own lives to save others in the First World War – they are pictured aboard their lifeboat *Bob Newbon*.

Many ships in the North Sea, the English Channel and the Atlantic were targeted by German U-boats, and lifeboat crews were called out to unfamiliar situations, such as ships carrying large numbers of passengers that had been torpedoed or struck mines. This would sometimes include the distressing job of recovering bodies. The sinking of the passenger liner RMS *Lusitania* off County Cork in May 1915 caused the deaths of over 1,000 people – Courtmacsherry lifeboat volunteers were among those who helped recover the bodies. There were also calls to ships on official war duty, such as the hospital ship *Rohilla*. Six lifeboat crews battled high seas and storm-force winds for 50 hours to save 144 lives (there's more on *Rohilla* and how *Henry Vernon* – one of the first motorised lifeboats – helped, on page 20).

It soon became clear that over £500,000 was needed to modernise the lifeboat fleet – around £27 million in today's money.

Other First World War rescues included the safe return of 14 people from a boat sunk by a German submarine, rescued by lifeboat volunteers at Fraserburgh, Aberdeenshire. In Falmouth, Cornwall, lifeboat volunteers rescued 19 sailors from SS *Pontus*, which had run aground. At Clacton-on-Sea in Essex, 27 lives were saved from *Gorliz* of Bilbao and another vessel. And the crew of Gorleston in Norfolk rescued two vessels – *La France* of Kragerø and *Seaconnel* of Philadelphia – saving 44.

In all, over 5,000 lives were saved at sea by lifeboat volunteers during the First World War. But it wasn't until the fighting stopped that the true extent of the RNLI's contribution to the war effort came into view. Until then, information blackouts had stopped news of their work from being publicised. The impact of the war on the RNLI – not least its lifeboats and equipment – led to concerns in high places about its future. Once the Armistice had been signed in November 1918, it soon became clear that over £500,000 was needed to modernise the lifeboat fleet – around £27 million in today's money.

Admiral Wemyss, the senior British representative at the Armistice, later said: 'This raising of half a million must be the cause of great anxiety to the RNLI. We know how people's pockets are strained at this moment, and how many things there are to which they can give their charity, but surely there are not many that are greater than this.'

His concerns must have had an impact, as by 1919 the RNLI began an ambitious motor lifeboat building programme. Following the success of *Henry Vernon* in the rescue of the survivors of *Rohilla*, 50 new motor lifeboats were added to the fleet. No one could have known at the time how soon these new lifeboats would be called upon to help in a second global conflict.

Second World War

As war began to rage across Europe in 1939, planes were regularly downed in the water, pilots from both sides being left to the mercy of the sea. RNLI lifeboats were launched frequently to rescue airmen and their passengers, no matter what side they were on.

As in the First World War, the average age of the lifeboat crews crept up since men of fighting age were sent overseas to fight.

Lifeboats were launched almost 4,000 times between 1939 and 1945, most often to come to the aid of ships caught in the conflict. Over 6,000 lives were saved and 134 Medals for Gallantry were awarded. But among all of the stories of gallantry and incredible courage, it is perhaps the Dunkirk evacuation and the part played by lifeboat volunteers that best reflect the institution's contribution to the war effort.

Dunkirk spirit

The rescue operation staged by the British Navy at Dunkirk in northern France changed the course of the war. On 30 May 1940, alongside 700 private boats, 19 RNLI lifeboats sailed from lifeboat stations on the south-east coast of England to Dunkirk as part of Operation Dynamo. Their mission: to help rescue some of the more than 338,000 British and French soldiers who were trapped on the beaches by advancing German forces.

The Allied soldiers had only one escape route, via the eastern beaches near Dunkirk. Because the waters were too shallow for large ships to get close enough, the plan with Operation Dynamo was to gather as many 'little ships' as possible to speedily collect the soldiers from the beaches. The Admiralty rapidly assembled a fleet of small boats: pleasure boats, barges, fishing boats, schooners and, of course, as many lifeboats as they could.

Little ships, courageous crews

While most of the commandeered lifeboats were crewed by members of the armed forces rather than lifeboat volunteers, the crews of Ramsgate and Margate RNLI on the Kent coast took part in the operation. It would be their greatest challenge. Setting sail for France, they had onboard some unfamiliar equipment: steel helmets, gas masks, grass towing warp, and extra supplies of fuel and fresh drinking water. Their orders: to bring soldiers off the beaches and into the safety of the rescue ships waiting offshore.

Ramsgate's lifeboat *Prudential* arrived at Malo-les-Bains, two miles east of Dunkirk, in the black of night. The boat towed behind it a row of small workboats known as 'wherries'. More normally seen nipping about on the Thames, they were ideal for getting close to shore and rescuing the waiting soldiers.

Under enemy fire and against strong tides, a number of Ramsgate's lifeboatmen helped row the wherries to the beach to collect soldiers, while the rest of the crew held the lifeboat steady. The crews faced a tough row through the surf to get the soldiers out to the lifeboat, which was then used to ferry them to a bigger motorboat waiting further out.

By daybreak, the wind had started to come in off the sea and the lifeboat's oars were weighed down with oil. It became impossible to row the wherries through the surf. So, instead of fighting the elements, the crew used them to their advantage. They allowed the wherries to drift inshore, propelled by the onshore wind, then hauled them back to the lifeboat using ropes.

'The average age of the lifeboat crews crept up, since men of fighting age were sent to fight'

Lifeboat volunteers kept going for 30 hours until the last of the wherries, battered by the surf, was too damaged to continue. Even then, the work of the crew didn't stop. After a long trek back across the channel to Ramsgate, the crew were in action again on home shores, bringing injured troops ashore from other vessels.

Ramsgate's 14m motor lifeboat *Prudential* was built in 1925 in Cowes, Isle of Wight, and was designed to save lives off the coast of the UK. But 15 years later the lifeboat would help evacuate soldiers from France in the Dunkirk evacuations.

Margate's lifeboat *Lord Southborough (Civil Service No.1)* was one of the few crewed by lifeboat volunteers during the Dunkirk evacuation. Former Margate Coxswain Stephen Clayson is pictured with the lifeboat.

Meanwhile, Margate's lifeboat volunteers and their lifeboat *Lord Southborough (Civil Service No.1)* had been towed across the Channel by a Dutch barge to conserve fuel. They reached Nieuport – a Belgian town 15 miles east of Dunkirk – a few hours after the Ramsgate lifeboat arrived at Malo-les-Bains.

Shells burst and fires raged in the darkness and the chaos, but the crew got to work quickly, carrying troops from the shore to the Dutch barge. When that was full, the crew brought the soldiers to the Royal Navy destroyer HMS *Icarus*. But finding themselves under attack from enemy planes above, the Margate lifeboat crew made the difficult decision that carrying on would cost more lives than they could save, and began their journey home.

Over 338,000 people were rescued between 26 May and 4 June, of which over a third were evacuated by Dunkirk's 'little ships' and the lifeboats that were part of them.

'Giving no thought to past tragedies or immediate danger'

In 1944 the Canadian frigate *Chebogue* suffered heavy casualties when her stern was blown away by an enemy torpedo, leaving her stranded in dangerous waters. She was towed to the apparent safety of Swansea Bay, but unfortunately the weather took a dramatic turn for the worse.

In 1883 and 1903 Mumbles lifeboats had capsized and lost crew during two particularly violent storms. One crew member from 1903 was aboard the lifeboat that went to the aid of the *Chebogue*. Giving no thought to past tragedies or immediate danger, the crew launched into darkness, sleet and enormous waves towards the damaged frigate.

In an extraordinary feat of seamanship and bravery, Coxswain William Gammon drove full speed over the bar to reach the seaward side of the wreckage and then held the boat still just long enough for some crew to make the dangerous leap aboard. Coxswain Gammon repeated this remarkable manoeuvre 12 times, rescuing all 42 of the frigate's crew, with only a few suffering minor injuries from the life-or-death leap onto the lifeboat.

The fact that crew of the Mumbles had an average age of 55 – with two crew members over 60 and two more over 70 – makes this rescue all the more remarkable. For his actions, Coxswain William Gammon was awarded the Gold Medal for Gallantry, with Second Coxswain Tom Ace and Mechanic Gilbert Davies receiving the Bronze Medal.

This painting by Tim Thompson depicts the rescue carried out by Mumbles lifeboat volunteers in 1944, leading to crew members receiving three medals for gallantry.

A hero among heroes: Henry Blogg

One man, who served on the Cromer lifeboat during both wars, stands out for his unerring courage and incredible longevity.

Henry Blogg joined the lifeboat crew at 18 years old, became coxswain 15 years later and remained coxswain for a further 38 years. Henry was awarded many honours, including three Gold and four Silver Medals from the RNLI, the George Cross for general war service and a British Empire Medal. To this day, he remains the most decorated crew member in RNLI history.

In 1917, during the First World War, Henry and his crew launched four times in 14 hours in a terrible storm. Cromer's lifeboat, *Louisa Heartwell*, battled high winds to rescue the 22 crew onboard the Greek vessel *Pyrin*. The Cromer crew, which like so many in the wartime RNLI had an average age of over 50 – with two members over 70 – had to rely on 14 oars and two sails to navigate the heavy seas.

LEFT: Henry Blogg was often seen with his dog Monte, a Tyrolean mountain dog he rescued from an Italian steamship. See the next chapter for more animal rescue tales.

ABOVE: The crew of Cromer's lifeboat, *Louisa Heartwell*, raise their oars during lauching. You can see *Louisa Heartwell* at the Historic Lifeboat Collection, Chatham Historic Dockyard.

As the exhausted crew arrived back on shore, they were alerted to the plight of the Swedish ship *Fernebo*, which had been blown in half by a sea mine. They rowed out three times to rescue the sailors onboard. Henry, who was awarded his first Gold Medal for the rescue, was commended for his 'remarkable personality' and 'admirable leadership', and the crew were awarded Bronze Medals.

Visit the Henry Blogg Museum

Henry Blogg served a remarkable 53 years on the lifeboat and retired at the grand age of 74. His unique contribution to both saving lives during wartime and to Cromer's lifesaving story is commemorated in the museum named after him. The Henry Blogg Museum is situated at the end of the promenade in Cromer, and is home to the lifeboat stationed at Cromer during the Second World War.

Visitors to the Henry Blogg Museum in Cromer can see *HF Bailey*, the lifeboat that he powered to the rescue for decades.

Henry Blogg saved lives aboard Cromer lifeboats during both world wars. He remains the most decorated lifeboat crew member in the RNLI's history.

Twenty-five years later, in 1932, the Italian steamship *Monte Nevoso* ran aground on the Haisborough Sands off the Norfolk coast. Cromer's lifeboat launched with several tugs to refloat the ship, but after several hours it began to break up. The crew were taken off, but the officers onboard refused to leave. Henry determinedly returned to the ship twice for the captain and his officers, but they still refused, and on his third trip he found the ship abandoned, with the officers presumed lost. Left behind were a Tyrolean mountain dog and a number of caged birds, which Henry duly rescued. Henry had been at sea for 52 hours by the time he got home. He was awarded a Silver Medal for the rescue and given the rescued dog, whom he renamed Monte.

The fallout from mines and air attacks in the Second World War kept the Cromer lifeboat crew and Henry Blogg very busy. After the war ended, Cromer counted the lives they had saved. Having launched 150 times, they saved 448 lives – more than any other lifeboat crew.

To save every one

Our amazing volunteer lifeboat crews continue to launch to the aid of anyone who is in trouble in or around the water and needs our help. We have done this since the RNLI was founded in 1824, and during the course of two world wars. This will always be our ethos. We do not judge a casualty on the circumstances that have found them in trouble. Our crews are tasked by HM Coastguard in the UK and the Irish Coast Guard in Ireland to rescue anyone who is at risk. When our lifeboats launch, we operate under International Maritime Law, which states that we are permitted and indeed obligated to enter all waters regardless of territories for search and rescue purposes. We do not question why casualties got into trouble, nor who they are or where they come from. All we need to know is that they need our help.

RNLI volunteers go home after a shout secure in the knowledge that without their help, the people they rescued may not have been able to be reunited with their own family. That is why our volunteers do what they do. Our crews will never judge those we rescue – where we believe there is a risk to life at sea, we will do all we can to save it.

Our crews do what they do because they believe that anyone can drown, but no one should. They believe in and remain focused on our core purpose – along with every member of the RNLI – to save lives at sea.

'Our crews launch to the aid of anyone in trouble in or around the water. We have done this since the RNLI was founded … and during the course of two world wars'

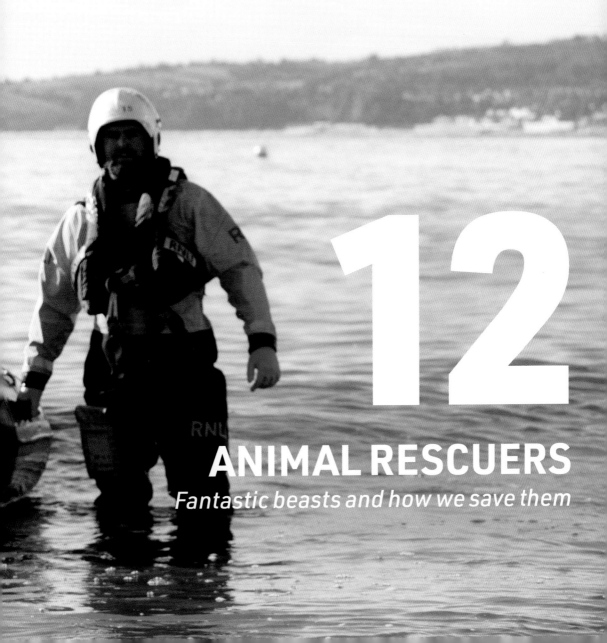

12

ANIMAL RESCUERS

Fantastic beasts and how we save them

It's not only human lives that our volunteers are called upon to save. Many of the rescues our volunteers respond to involve much-loved pets, wildlife and livestock. How do animals get into these situations? And why do our volunteers give their time and energy, sometimes putting their own lives at risk, to rescue them? The answers to these questions are not always straightforward.

Every rescue tells a different story and the circumstances that lead to animal rescues are each as unique as the animals themselves. Whether it's a dog who has fallen from a cliff edge, a dolphin who has lost its way or a sheep who has wandered into the water, how animals come to need rescuing is never the important thing to us. RNLI volunteers are always concerned with the safety of people who are at risk of drowning. Very often where animals are at risk, so too are humans. Pet owners, farmers or concerned passers-by will often try to enter the water to rescue an animal; it's an entirely natural reflex any animal lover can identify with. But far too often this type of situation has led to tragedy.

As skilled lifesavers with the training and equipment to cope in any number of rescue situations, it is always safer for an RNLI volunteer to help an animal in distress than to allow others to attempt to rescue it.

Lucky hounds rescued by the RNLI include Yogi the spaniel, who fell down a cliff. Devon's Torbay lifeboat crew members went to his aid.

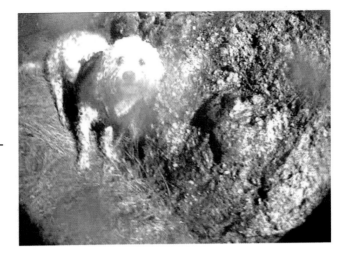

Moelfre lifeboat volunteers headed to the rescue of Flossy the Bichon Frise after she got trapped on a ledge above the sea on the Conwy coast.

Man's best friends

Whether they've swum out too far, found themselves trapped by the tides or fallen from unfamiliar cliffs while on holiday, dogs in danger of drowning have always been the animals our crews and lifeguards are asked to help most often. In 2022 the RNLI rescued 164 dogs.

Flossy the survivor

In 2017 Flossy the Bichon Frise-Shih Tzu mix was enjoying a holiday walk in Anglesey with her owners Clare and Terry and their daughter Beatrice, when she disappeared over a grassy mound. Clare called her to come back, but when Flossy didn't return as usual the family realised very quickly that something was wrong.

Flossy had lost her footing while inspecting the grassy mound and had fallen an astonishing 130ft. She was now trapped on a ledge in an isolated cove with no way for her to climb back up. Clare dialled 999 and asked for the coastguard, who quickly arrived to help. But it became clear that it was too dangerous for them to attempt to get to the cove via land and that the only way to reach Flossy would be from the water.

The coastguard called the volunteer crew from Moelfre RNLI, who happened to be on a training exercise, and they made their way to the cove. A lifeboat crew member went ashore and coaxed a confused, cold and tired Flossy into their arms, and the beloved pet was reunited with her owners.

Lucky cats

There's a long tradition of taking cats on ships – they were used in the past to keep mice and rats under control, and our archives tell of several ships' captains who were rescued with their cats in their arms. But today most RNLI cat rescues involve domestic moggies who have found themselves in tricky situations.

Icicle the cat was treated to a fish supper after being rescued from a Norfolk river by Great Yarmouth and Gorleston lifeboat volunteers.

Icicle swims to safety

A white cat named Icicle was rescued by volunteer crew members from Great Yarmouth and Gorleston RNLI in Norfolk in 2022. The all-white moggy had fallen from a wall while walking along the River Bure and was clinging on to the side of the wall just above the waterline by the skin of his claws. A member of the public saw Icicle, who was meowing loudly, and wisely decided to call the RNLI rather than try to attempt a rescue themselves.

The crew of the lifeboat *John Rowntree* sped to Icicle's aid and were astonished to see the brave cat begin to swim towards the lifeboat as they approached him. Icicle was wrapped up in warm blankets and given a fish supper by the crew before being returned to his owner, Mandy.

'The crew of the lifeboat were astonished to see the brave cat swim towards the lifeboat'

Livestock as well as pets and wild animals have been rescued by our crews, including this sheep that leapt into the sea after being chased by a dog. Luckily Hoylake RNLI hovercraft crew went to the rescue – Crew Member Emily Jones is pictured with the woolly jumper.

Unusual animals

While dogs are the animals we rescue most often, our lifeguards and lifeboat crews regularly rescue some less commonly domesticated creatures. Whether it's digging a horse out of mud or beckoning cheeky ferrets back to safety, our volunteers have to think quickly in some pretty unlikely situations to help animals in peril.

Whale

In 1857 the crew of the lifeboat at Tynemouth were called out to rescue a stranded whale that was stuck on the rocks near the mouth of the Tyne. The bottlenose whale was 40ft long and in danger of drowning. Owing to their huge size and weight, when whales get stranded on beaches or in shallow water, their organs become compromised and it's increasingly difficult for them to breathe. The crew managed to secure a line to the whale and used their boat to pull it back into the safety of deeper water, where it swam away.

Cow

In 1923 the RNLI lifeboat at Port St Mary, Isle of Man, rescued a cow that had fallen off a cliff and was stranded on a rocky beach below. The lifeboat crew used ropes to hoist the cow back up the cliff to safety.

Seal

In 1950 a baby seal was found stranded on the beach at Frinton and, according to the *Lifeboat* magazine of the time, was adopted by Coxswain WJ Oxley of the Walton and Frinton lifeboat.

Deer

Cowes lifeboat crew, based on the Isle of Wight, were training on a July morning in 2021 when they spotted a deer in the waves. The Muntjac deer, a species commonly found in Hampshire's New Forest, had appeared to have been carried three miles out to sea by the tide. The young deer was carefully pulled aboard, wrapped in a blanket and taken back to the lifeboat station for a drink – before being handed into the care of the RSPCA.

Terrapin

In 2020 lifeguards at Perranporth Beach in Cornwall dealt with a terrapin that had been missing from its owners for six weeks. The terrapin had escaped and travelled downstream for almost two miles before being picked up by a member of the public and handed to the RNLI lifeguards at Perranporth.

Ferrets

In 2013 lifeboat volunteers from Newbiggin in Northumberland conducted what is thought to be the RNLI's first and only ferret rescue. Two adventurous ferrets, Tootsie and the aptly named Lucky, were stranded on rocks off the coast of Cambois and in danger of drowning as the tide rose rapidly around them. Newbiggin RNLI crew rescued the pair in the nick of time, after their anxious owners put in a 999 call to Humber coastguard.

Dolphins

In March 2023 the RNLI hovercraft at Hoylake and New Brighton's inshore lifeboat helped two dolphins when they became stranded and injured on a sandbank on the River Mersey. Lifeboat volunteers worked with marine mammal medics to help the pair – a mother and her calf – back to the safety of the river.

13

MODERN LIFEBOATS
Propellers, waterjets and how we got faster

As the RNLI entered its second century of saving lives at sea, the needs of our lifeboat crews – and of the people whose lives they continued to save – began to change. Two world wars had seen many of the lifeboats commandeered by the Admiralty (read more about the RNLI in wartime on page 132), and slowed down any major developments in lifeboat design and production. But as the 20th century progressed – with air travel, holidays and leisure-time by the sea or on inland waterways becoming commonplace – we continued to innovate, creating new, improved lifeboats for our volunteer crews.

PREVIOUS PAGE: Arran RNLI volunteers power their Atlantic 85 lifeboat through the seas off the west coast of Ireland.

Our lifeboats became faster and more powerful, reducing response times and saving more lives as a result. They also became increasingly bespoke to the area they were serving and the needs of the people using the water there. But whether we've been developing pioneering inflatable lifeboats for inshore rescues or building the fastest-ever carriage-launching boat, the aim has always been to give our crews the best possible tools for their vital work.

Dover's groundbreaking motorised lifeboat *Sir William Hillary* was named after the RNLI's founder. With its top speed of 18 knots and onboard electric equipment, it was a far cry from the purpose-built lifeboats first funded by the RNLI some 100 years earlier.

The first fast motorised lifeboat

By the 1930s air travel was well established, and the increasing number of aircraft flying over the English Channel meant more and more aircraft came down at sea.

In Dover the lifeboat station had been closed for most of the 1920s as the station's cumbersome steam-powered lifeboat required the expertise of a technical crew that was no longer available after the First World War.

But by 1930 the station was ready to re-open, with the RNLI's first fast motor lifeboat at its heart. *Sir William Hillary* – named after the charity's founder – was designed to rapidly reach casualties in the Channel. Moored afloat to ensure minimal launch time, it was powered by two 375hp petrol engines and had a top speed of 18 knots, making the boat nearly twice as fast as any other motor lifeboats in the fleet at the time.

But it wasn't only about speed. The 64ft lifeboat was the first to have an onboard electric supply, which provided light for the crew and powered a wireless radio, searchlight, throwline night tracers and a Morse Code signalling lamp. There was also a cabin onboard for the first time, giving crew protection against the weather. Waterjets could extinguish fires – common in rescues involving aircraft – and there was room for as many as 50 casualties onboard.

The crew of *Sir William Hillary* received gallantry awards and Thanks of the Institution Inscribed on Vellum for rescuing 16 crew members from the former fishing boat *Blackburn Rovers*. The trawler was on anti-submarine patrol in the Channel in November 1939 when it began drifting into enemy minefields, its screw propeller having become entangled in one of its own cables, rendering it helpless.

Sir William Hillary was commandeered by the Admiralty in 1940 and it served as an air-sea rescue vessel throughout the rest of the Second World War, as well as helping with commando training.

'*Sir William Hillary* – named after the RNLI's founder – was designed to rapidly reach casualties in the Channel'

Introducing inflatable lifeboats

By the mid-20th century the domestic holiday market had begun to flourish, and with a general rise in prosperity came an uptick in leisure time and more people spending time at the beach. As a result, there was a need for quicker, more agile lifeboats that could help crews reach the areas where people were using the water, closer to beaches and the cliffs and caves of the coastline. Inflatable lifeboats were introduced in 1963 and have remained integral to the RNLI fleet ever since.

The early inflatable lifeboats were constructed using a tough nylon material proofed with neoprene and powered by a 40hp outboard motor engine. They could reach speeds of 20 knots or more with two crew members onboard, and two more were needed to help launch.

Rigid inflatable boats (RIBs) came along in the early 1970s. The B class Atlantic 21 lifeboat (named after Atlantic College in Wales, where it was first developed) served lifeboat stations in the UK and Ireland between 1972 and 2006. These 7m, 32-knot vessels were the first generation of RIBs:

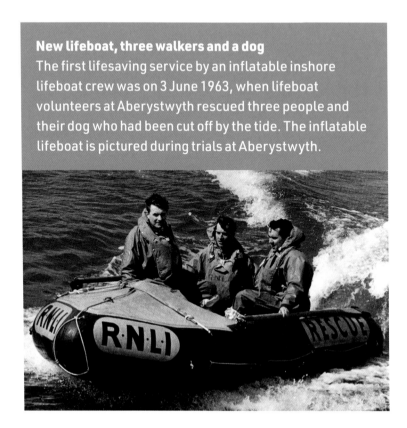

New lifeboat, three walkers and a dog
The first lifesaving service by an inflatable inshore lifeboat crew was on 3 June 1963, when lifeboat volunteers at Aberystwyth rescued three people and their dog who had been cut off by the tide. The inflatable lifeboat is pictured during trials at Aberystwyth.

faster, more manoeuvrable and with greater reliability than the existing inflatables. The B class evolved to include the Atlantic 75 (introduced in 1993) and the Atlantic 85 (introduced in 2005), named for their respective lengths of about 7.5m and 8.5m.

Today's B class and the smaller D class inflatable lifeboats are state of the art, and their onboard equipment includes fitted and hand-held VHF radio, night-vision equipment, first aid kit and oxygen. Because they're lighter and smaller than our all-weather boats, you'll see them being launched mostly by a davit system or a trolley on the beach.

All-weather lifeboats

In the 1990s the RNLI set out to bring its all-weather lifeboat fleet – the craft that could withstand the worst conditions – up to a standard speed of 25 knots. Since then, several new classes of all-weather lifeboat have gradually replaced their slower, but well-loved predecessors, such as the 17-knot Tyne class lifeboats. Wicklow lifeboat crew waved goodbye to the last Tyne class in service in 2019 (pictured overleaf).

The last Tyne class lifeboat *Annie Blaker* was officially retired from the RNLI in 2019 at Wicklow Lifeboat Station, after 30 years of service there. The Tyne class lifeboats were first introduced into the RNLI fleet in 1982, with the final one built in 1990.

FOCUS ON: MODERN LIFEBOATS

Mersey

The Mersey class all-weather lifeboat was designed for locations where only a beach launch is possible. As the RNLI's first fast carriage-launch lifeboat it is capable of 17.5 knots, and the lightweight, 12m-long boat can also operate off a slipway or lie afloat on a mooring. Its propellers and rudders lie in partial tunnels set into the hull, and these – along with two bilge keels – provide protection from damage in shallow waters or slipway launches. Its mast and aerials can collapse down to ensure the boat fits into a boathouse.

Trent and Severn

By the late 1980s the lifesaving success of lifeboats with higher speeds and more rapid responses had been proven time and time again, so the RNLI set itself the ambitious goal of replacing its all-weather lifeboats with new, faster designs by 1993, when many of the early motorised lifeboats were due for replacement.

The state of the art, all-weather Trent and Severn class boats were built to provide the quickest possible response times and travel further out to sea – up to 50 miles – than any of their predecessors.

The Trent class's first active service was at Alderney Lifeboat Station in 1994. The boat is designed to lie afloat for a fast launch time and the low line of the hull makes recovering casualties much easier for our crews.

Similar in capabilities to the Trent, the Severn class is larger and better able to tow larger vessels to safety. Both classes of lifeboats have daughter boats for accessing hard-to-reach places, together with a portable salvage pump to help sinking boats.

Tamar

While the Severn and Trent class lifeboats had been in the fleet for years by the start of the 21st century, the RNLI still lacked a slipway-launched all-weather lifeboat capable of reaching 25 knots. This all changed with the development of the Tamar class lifeboat. And it wasn't just speed that the new craft offered – it was the first of our lifeboats to be fitted with an integrated electronic systems and information management system (SIMS), enabling the crew to operate the lifeboat from the safety of their shock-absorbing seats, increasing their safety and reducing the strain on their backs.

While the Tamar is designed to be launched from a slipway and is kept in a boathouse (the mast and aerials can be lowered to fit inside), it can also lie afloat. Tamar class lifeboats have gradually replaced our Tyne class lifeboats, which have reached the end of their operational lives.

Shannon

The Shannon is the first modern all-weather lifeboat to be propelled by waterjets instead of traditional propellers, making it our most agile and manoeuvrable all-weather lifeboat yet. It was designed entirely in-house by our team at the All-weather Lifeboat Centre in Poole, and builds on the pioneering systems used in the Tamar, to ensure the fastest and safest rescues possible.

In February 2023, the RNLI's oldest serving all-weather lifeboat *Doris M Mann of Ampthill* (known to her crew as simply Doris) was retired after almost 33 years of service at Wells-next-the Sea in Norfolk. It was replaced by a new Shannon class lifeboat, named *Duke of Edinburgh*.

D class

With a top speed of 25 knots, our inshore D class lifeboats can endure three hours at sea at this speed on search and rescue missions – a crucial factor when lives are at risk. They can access

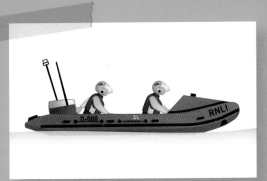

areas inaccessible to our all-weather lifeboats, such as close to cliffs, rocks and inside caves, and can operate in big surf.

In the event of a capsize, the D class lifeboat can be righted manually by the crew, and the 50hp outboard engine restarted. With over 50 years' service, our D class lifeboat has helped us save thousands of lives at sea and continues to be the workhorse of the RNLI fleet today.

B class Atlantic 85

When it comes to racing to the scene, our inshore B class Atlantic 85 lifeboat is one of the fastest in the fleet; her top speed is 35 knots, powered by two 115hp 4-stroke engines. Although she's an inshore lifeboat, designed to operate in shallower water, the B class can handle fairly challenging open-sea conditions too – near gale Force 7 winds in daylight and Force 6 at night.

There's a manually operated righting mechanism in the event of a capsize, which involves inflating a bag on top of the roll bar. And the lifeboat's engines are inversion-proofed so that they will shut down in a capsize (and can be restarted after being righted).

E class

With its powerful tidal currents, submerged debris and heavy traffic, the River Thames can be incredibly dangerous for those on and by the water, and the E class lifeboat was designed to handle these river conditions.

Stationed at our two busiest lifeboat stations, Tower and Chiswick, the first generation of E class lifeboats – the Mk1 – was introduced into the fleet in 2002 and the second generation – the Mk2 – in 2012.

Waterjets give our 40-knot E class lifeboat excellent manoeuvrability in the rapidly moving river flow, when alongside other craft and in confined waters.

The foredeck is long enough for a stretcher or crew to resuscitate casualties. The aft-deck open transom extension allows casualties to be recovered quickly, crew to re-board unassisted, and provides protection over the waterjets.

The collar on the Mk2 E class is an innovative teardrop shape, aiding man-overboard recovery. The higher-density foam increases robustness and the flattened bow means she can push casualty vessels or approach pontoons and quaysides bow on without damaging the collar.

Why do we name our lifeboats after rivers?
The first all-weather lifeboat class to be named after a river was the Tyne class, after a coxswain from Tynemouth who was involved in its design. The tradition of naming our lifeboats after rivers has stuck ever since.

Hovercraft

Mudflats and sandbanks can be especially dangerous places. People and animals risk getting caught out by quicksand, mud and rising tides, but the terrain is too soft for land vehicles to go to the rescue and the water is too shallow for boats.

The introduction of the rescue hovercraft to our lifeboat fleet in 2002 instantly created quicker, easier access – and an increased capacity for searching – to mudflats and sandbanks at four lifeboat stations in England: Morecambe, Hoylake, Hunstanton and Southend-on-Sea.

A hovercraft lifts up with two fans that build up air pressure underneath, and two large fans mounted on the back act in the same way as aeroplane propellers, thrusting the vehicle forward. It's for this reason that hovercraft are the only lifeboats in the RNLI fleet to have pilots, not coxswains.

Pilots steer the craft by rudders at the rear. When it reaches a casualty, the crew of the hovercraft are able to easily settle the craft alongside the scene and the skirt provides a soft edge for recovering casualties.

For more on our Thames lifesavers, see page 192.

Morecambe RNLI hovercraft *The Hurley Flyer* during a training exercise.

A cleaner future

As we enter our third century of saving lives at sea, we're committed to reducing the emissions we create and the impact the RNLI fleet has on climate change.

We're not there yet, but we're working on the application of alternative propulsion technologies to our boats and launching vehicles. While there aren't any practical solutions ready to implement today that can support our operational needs in terms of speed and range, shoreside infrastructure and safety, we're continuing to work with industrial and academic partners to explore a range of options including hybrid electric, fuel cells, methanol and hydrogen.

In the meantime, all of our lifeboat crews are being encouraged to go a bit slower when life is not in immediate danger. A small reduction in speed can lead to a large reduction in greenhouse gas emissions. And we'll continue to closely track the changes in available fuels, mobile energy sources, energy infrastructure and marine engine technologies, trialling and testing where we can, to ensure a cleaner future for our fleet.

Like all Shannon class lifeboats, Girvan's all-weather craft is powered through the waves using waterjets rather than propellers. The Shannon is the newest and most sophisticated class of all-weather RNLI lifeboat.

'We'll continue to closely track the changes in fuels, energy sources, infrastructure and technologies ... to ensure a cleaner future for our fleet'

14

LAUNCHING
LEGENDS

The hidden heroes behind every rescue

Lifeboats and their crews might do the hard work of search and rescue, but how does a lifeboat get into the water and who makes that happen? The solutions are every bit as challenging, complex and varied as the coastline itself.

The first launchers

Brave RNLI volunteers have been launching lifeboats for 200 years. Those crews who could not launch lifeboats down slipways relied on human strength and horsepower to reach the sea in the RNLI's first century. Because the men were needed on the lifeboat, and because there was still a lot of superstition about women on lifeboats, it was sometimes women who heaved the boats to the sea, battling the elements in their skirts to get the boat to the water. You can read all about the 'lady launchers' who made sure the lifeboat got into the sea on page 52.

A remarkable feat of endurance in January 1899 saw volunteers and horses pull the Lynmouth lifeboat 13 miles to the safest launching spot at Porlock, Somerset. The overland launch was re-enacted 100 years later (pictured).

But as well as the strength of female launchers, lifeboat volunteers also relied on horses to help them get their boats afloat, the animals playing a crucial part in saving thousands of lives at sea. In villages and towns around the coast, these magnificent beasts were always an impressive sight as they pulled the lifeboat through the streets and beaches and into the sea to launch to those in trouble. When the call for help came, horses were hired locally – usually from local farmers – to pull the lifeboat on a wheeled carriage across often vast, tricky terrain and get the lifeboat into the water.

Send for the horses: the Porlock launch of 1899

One of the most extraordinary lifeboat launches ever recorded involved 18 horses and almost 100 helpers. In January 1899 the 1,900-tonne ship *Forrest Hall* was caught in a violent storm near Lynmouth on the north Devon and Somerset coast. The high winds and torrential rain meant it was impossible for the lifeboat to launch, so the coxswain and his crew decided to carry the lifeboat 13 miles overland to the shelter of the harbour at Porlock Weir, where launching would be possible. The journey took 11 hours and included a 400m climb up Countisbury Hill. Along with scores of helpers and the lifeboat crew, 18 horses dragged the Lynmouth lifeboat *Louisa* through the night to Porlock. Once there, the crew immediately launched the lifeboat and were able to rescue all 18 crew of the stricken *Forrest Hall*. This incredible effort remains one of the most difficult launches in RNLI history, and it couldn't have happened without the horses who pulled the boat to Porlock.

'Lifeboat volunteers also relied on horses to help them get their boats afloat ... the animals playing a crucial part in saving thousands of lives at sea'

Most Shannon class lifeboats are
launched and recovered on beaches
using a powerful mobile slipway.
Lancashire's Lytham St Annes
Shannon class lifeboat is pictured
being recovered by the Shannon
Launch and Recovery System
(SLARS) after a training exercise

A new era

At the start of the First World War many horses were commandeered by the military, so lifeboat launches by horse became rarer. The decline in agriculture also meant fewer available horses and farmers were reluctant to allow their use in case of injury. So at some lifeboat stations it was impossible to hire any at all, while at others they had to be brought from so far away that launches were considerably delayed. In 1920 trials involving a 3-tonne 35hp Clayton and Shuttleworth caterpillar tractor with a top speed of 6mph proved successful. The tractor pulled Hunstanton Lifeboat Station's 7.5-tonne lifeboat and carriage over the flat sands, sand dunes and uneven, rocky ground of Hunstanton Beach with ease. A lifeboat launch that would usually require up to 10 horses and the same number of volunteer helpers took just one tractor and four helpers. More importantly, pulling the lifeboat 200m across the steep part of the beach to the sea took just seven minutes. This was a radical reduction in launch time that would help save more lives.

This tractor, pictured being trialled at Hunstanton in Norfolk, was a game-changer when it came to launching lifeboats – tractors would soon replace horses when it came to getting crews into the sea.

Other ways to launch a lifeboat

Powering a lifeboat across a beach is just one way of launching. There are all sorts of solutions, depending on station locations and local terrain and topography – from slipways to pontoons. Some inland stations such as Rhyl launch their inshore lifeboats (ILBs) with a Land Rover, while at Workington Lifeboat Station the all-weather lifeboat is launched by a crane-like davit system over the dock wall.

In stations where some of the largest all-weather lifeboats are stationed, such as Harwich, home to a Severn class all-weather lifeboat and a B class Atlantic 85 ILB, the all-weather lifeboat lies afloat, next to a pontoon berth.

The Harwich lifeboat in Essex lies afloat, so crew members like the station's Coxswain Di Bush can simply step aboard and power out to sea.

FOCUS ON: HIDDEN HEROES

Today there are over 10 types of lifeboat-launching machines in the RNLI fleet, each one adapted for launching different kinds of lifeboats in all kinds of coastal terrain around the UK and Ireland.

Let's take a closer look:

TALUS MB-4H
(AKA: BENDY)

LAUNCHES: *B CLASS LIFEBOAT*

MAX WADING DEPTH	1.1m
WEIGHT	9.4 tonnes
NUMBER IN FLEET	31

IN SERVICE AT:

LIFEBOAT STATIONS	28
RELIEF FLEET	3

HAGGLUND BV 206
(AKA: BV)

LAUNCHES: *D CLASS LIFEBOAT*

MAX WADING DEPTH	80cm
WEIGHT	6.5 tonnes
NUMBER IN FLEET	2

IN SERVICE AT:

LIFEBOAT STATIONS	1
RELIEF FLEET	1

BOBCAT TRACKED LOADER
(AKA: BOBCAT)

LAUNCHES: *D CLASS LIFEBOAT*

MAX WADING DEPTH	20cm
WEIGHT	4.5 tonnes
NUMBER IN FLEET	8

IN SERVICE AT:

LIFEBOAT STATIONS	7
RELIEF FLEET	1

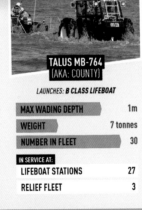

TALUS MB-764
(AKA: COUNTY)

LAUNCHES: *B CLASS LIFEBOAT*

MAX WADING DEPTH	1m
WEIGHT	7 tonnes
NUMBER IN FLEET	30

IN SERVICE AT:

LIFEBOAT STATIONS	27
RELIEF FLEET	3

SHANNON LAUNCH AND RECOVERY SYSTEM (AKA: SLRS)

LAUNCHES: *SHANNON CLASS LIFEBOAT*

MAX WADING DEPTH	2.4m
WEIGHT	37 tonnes
NUMBER IN FLEET	23

IN SERVICE AT:

LIFEBOAT STATIONS	19
RELIEF FLEET	4

TOOLTRAK

LAUNCHES: *D CLASS LIFEBOAT*

MAX WADING DEPTH	40cm
WEIGHT	1.3 tonnes
NUMBER IN FLEET	25

IN SERVICE AT:

LIFEBOAT STATIONS	18
RELIEF FLEET	7

SOFTRAK

LAUNCHES: *B AND D CLASS LIFEBOATS*

MAX WADING DEPTH	50cm
WEIGHT	2.5 tonnes
NUMBER IN FLEET	7

IN SERVICE AT:

LIFEBOAT STATIONS	5
RELIEF FLEET	2

TALUS MB-H
(AKA: CRAWLER)

LAUNCHES: *MERSEY AND B CLASS LIFEBOATS*

MAX WADING DEPTH	1.3m
WEIGHT	18.5 tonnes
NUMBER IN FLEET	12

IN SERVICE AT:

LIFEBOAT STATIONS	11
RELIEF FLEET	1

NEW HOLLAND SMALL AGRI TRACTOR (AKA: AGRI)

LAUNCHES: *D CLASS LIFEBOAT*

MAX WADING DEPTH	30cm
WEIGHT	1.6 tonnes
NUMBER IN FLEET	50

IN SERVICE AT:

LIFEBOAT STATIONS	39
RELIEF FLEET	11

LAND ROVER DEFENDER

LAUNCHES: *D CLASS LIFEBOAT*

MAX WADING DEPTH	30cm
WEIGHT	2 tonnes
NUMBER IN FLEET	36

IN SERVICE AT:

LIFEBOAT STATIONS	27
RELIEF FLEET	9

NEW HOLLAND LARGE AGRI TRACTOR (AKA: AGRI)

LAUNCHES: *B CLASS LIFEBOAT*

MAX WADING DEPTH	30cm
WEIGHT	4.2 tonnes
NUMBER IN FLEET	24

IN SERVICE AT:

LIFEBOAT STATIONS	21
RELIEF FLEET	3

Slipways

For many RNLI stations around the UK and Ireland's often craggy and perilous coastline, the lifeboat's journey into the water starts not with a tractor or a crane, but with a big slide down a slipway. Slipways enable stations to be built in places that are otherwise inaccessible for a boat due to rough terrain or a large tidal range. Some slipways are short and steep, others stretch out a long way, often over rocks and caves.

Padstow lifeboat launches down the station's slipway off the north Cornish coast.

Then and now

Mumbles Lifeboat Station at the south-western end of Swansea Bay is one of the busiest in Wales. In 2014 a new, fit-for-purpose boathouse and slipway were opened at the end of Mumbles pier. The old boathouse and slipway remain intact, however, providing a unique snapshot of how RNLI slipways have evolved over the last century. The 1922 clapboard station still has the RNLI badge on the door and is, along with the slipway, a Grade II listed building for its special interest as part of the cast-iron pier.

'For many RNLI stations, the lifeboat's journey into the water starts with a big slide down a slipway'

15

**ACTION
STATIONS**

Just as important as the lifeboats we design and build are the lifeboat stations where they're housed and in which our crews meet and train. There are currently 238 RNLI lifeboat stations creating a ring of safety around the UK and Ireland, and each station has its own unique features and functions.

Some house more than one lifeboat and many are located in extraordinary positions on the coast. Some are deeply rooted in the RNLI's past while others are buildings of the future. No two lifeboat stations are the same, but every one of our brilliant buildings plays a vital part in our work.

More than a mooring: what's in a lifeboat station?

Lifeboat stations are so much more than somewhere to keep the lifeboat, although providing shelter and safety for the lifeboat – or boats – when they're not in action is obviously one of their most important functions. Most stations have a central boathouse where the lifeboat is kept, and where RNLI mechanics carry out vital maintenance and repairs.

Lifeboat stations also provide a hub for the crew who meet and train there, so they also have communal space and kitchen facilities, changing rooms and drying rooms for kit.

Volunteers who don't go to sea but still need to spend time at the station, such as the lifeboat operations manager, also need space for administration. Not every station has everything they need yet – in some of our older stations, for example, changing facilities need updating and more space is needed for crew training. But we are working on ensuring every station is fit for purpose in the 21st century.

Some of our lifeboat stations, such as Tenby in Pembrokeshire and Wells in Norfolk, have viewing galleries where members of the public can watch the lifeboat and crew as they come in from an exercise or even when they launch for a rescue. Some, especially those located in popular tourist areas that get busy during holiday periods, also offer dedicated tours. Even when there's not a shout to get to, a lifeboat station can be a busy place, and viewing galleries are a great way to show the public the daily goings-on in the station. Many lifeboat stations also help raise funds thanks to their adjoining shops run by volunteers.

'Some of our stations have viewing galleries where the public can watch the lifeboat and crew'

Lifeguard huts like this one on La Braye Beach, Jersey have become some of the RNLI's most recognised – and essential – lifesaving buildings.

The long game:
sustainability in our stations

The RNLI aims to become more sustainable across everything we do and that includes our lifeboat stations. Designing our stations to be as energy efficient as possible and installing renewable energy sources where practical, all help to reduce our carbon footprint. We also consider the environmental impact of the materials we use both in construction and during use. This means we reduce our environmental impact and costs through life, ensuring that every penny of the funds we raise stretches further and lasts longer.

Our stations are working buildings housing lifeboats with lifespans of up to 50 years and we want them to have similar longevity, providing support and shelter for our crews well into the future. Many of the RNLI's stations are over 150 years of age and still in service, a testament to the

Aith Lifeboat Station and harbour at sunset, with the crew's Severn class lifeboat on the right and the RNLI wind turbine that helps source green energy.

original philosophies that have underpinned the charity since its foundation. If we can improve and upgrade old or historic stations, we do. In practice this can mean anything from fitting ground-source heat pumps to improving the overall insulation and energy efficiency (the new lifeboat station at Llandudno, for example, consumes no more energy than the much smaller building it replaced). Lifeboat stations have big doors that are frequently opened and they're therefore difficult buildings to heat efficiently. But we need dry, warm stations for our volunteer crew members, especially when they come in after a cold, wet shout. Our ground-source heat pumps work by drawing ambient temperature from the ground through a network of coiled pipes buried beneath the lifeboat station. This ambient heat is then passed through the heat pump, effectively making the station a fridge running in reverse. The pump condenses the heat energy, enabling us to heat the building and warm up wet crew members, all in a carbon-neutral way.

There are currently 28 ground-source heat pumps at various lifeboat stations and the Grace Darling Museum in Northumberland. We've also got 31 solar PV installations, and a wind turbine at Aith Lifeboat Station in Shetland. This is all helping to generate energy – as well as funds – for the charity and reduce its impact on the environment.

'This is all helping to generate energy – as well as funds – for the charity and reduce its impact on the environment'

FOCUS ON: PWLLHELI LIFEBOAT STATION

Adapting an old building for today's needs sometimes becomes unviable, and we need to design a building capable of meeting the needs of the crew and the lifeboat for the future. In 2020 this was the case for the lifeboat station at Pwllheli, on the Lleyn Peninsula.

This station brings together our operational and architectural gold standards in one place, providing a vision for the future of all our lifeboat stations.

Some of Pwllheli's highlights include:

- Climate-change adapted, featuring low, curved roofs with generous overhangs for shelter against the elements, all sitting above predicted rising tide levels and uncompromised access to the location at low and high tide, plus a sheltered launch area, making launching faster and safer for the crew
- Natural materials with indefinite or extensive lifespans, including copper for the roof, larch and composite boarding for cladding and limestone-faced walls
- Self-cleaning windows with solar-reflective glass
- Ground-source heating system providing warmth for all of the accommodation areas
- Photovoltaic panels on the south-facing roof providing electricity to offset the running costs of the pumps and lighting.

LARCH CLADDING

PHOTOVOLTAIC PANELS

LOW CURVED ROOFS

SELF-CLEANING WINDOWS

GROUND-SOURCE HEATING SYSTEM

ACCOYA TIMBER FRAMED WINDOWS

LIMESTONE-FACED WALLS

RNLI 13-39

A capital rescue service

One of the RNLI's most unusual lifeboat stations is also its busiest. Lifeboat crew at Tower, a floating station at Victoria Embankment on the Thames in London, respond to more calls and save more lives than at any other lifeboat station. Crew are on-site at Tower 24 hours a day and the Thames even has its own type of inshore lifeboat, the E class, a high-speed boat propelled by waterjets that was designed specifically for use on the capital's busy river.

The 1989 *Marchioness* tragedy, in which 51 people aboard a pleasure boat lost their lives after a collision with a dredger, highlighted the need for a dedicated rescue service on the River Thames. This led to the RNLI eventually setting up a rescue service on the river, with stations opened at Chiswick, Teddington, Gravesend and, in the heart of London, Tower.

After 20 years of saving lives in central London, Tower lifeboat crew got a new floating station, pictured being taken to its new home in 2023.

For more information on the E class and other inshore lifeboats, whizz over to page 220.

Not long after their new lifeboat station went operational in 2023, Tower was called to their 10,000th rescue. The crew that day were Neil Ceconi, Storm Smith-Suckoo, Laura Lewis and Suzanne Goldberg, pictured.

Tower RNLI's original floating station opened in 2002 and helped the crew save lives for more than 20 years before it was sailed out of service, having become unfit for purpose. It was built on a pontoon, parts of which dated back to Victorian times, and was cramped and uncomfortable, with little privacy for crew or casualties. The turbulent water of the Thames also caused a banging and jolting motion in the station, which had a considerable impact on the welfare of the crew.

The new state-of-the-art station at Tower is built with sustainability and energy efficiency at its core. It features what is believed to be the first small-scale water-source heat pump on the Thames and has solar PV panels on the roof. This reduces costs while optimising energy production and use.

The new station is positioned away from the river wall, using a bridge for access. This ensures greater privacy from passers-by, and stops the banging and jolting motion inside. The new station also has modern facilities, including a purpose-built space for casualty care, a drying room for kit and a new public engagement space for visitors. All steel used in the building was sourced from the EU, and the pontoon itself was made in Appledore on the Devon coast, not far from another RNLI station.

'The lifeboat crew at Tower, London, respond to more calls than any other lifeboat station'

Other brilliant buildings

In addition to our 238 lifeboat stations, the RNLI has a number of other important buildings, all of them vital to our lifesaving mission. Just as with our lifeboat stations, visitors and supporters are always welcome.

The RNLI College, Poole

The RNLI College in Poole, Dorset, is the home of RNLI training and was opened by Her Majesty Queen Elizabeth II on 28 July 2004 (when it was known as the Lifeboat College). This distinctive flagship building, with its wave-like roof and porthole windows, was first conceived as being a

As well as training lifesavers and hosting the public, the RNLI College is a venue for events, including our annual Women in Engineering day that welcomes students for an inspiring day of STEM activities.

The RNLI builds and
maintains its own
all-weather lifeboats
at a special facility
in Poole, Dorset.

training centre for lifeboat crews. We wanted to create a college of training excellence for our volunteers, an increasing number of whom were joining the RNLI without a maritime background. Since then, thousands of volunteer crew have passed through its doors and into its classrooms, lifeboats, live-engine workshops, bridge simulator and sea-survival pool. It's also become a popular place to stay in Poole, with 60 bedrooms overlooking Holes Bay in Poole Harbour. Guests get to rub shoulders with real-life RNLI lifeboat crew and lifeguards as they learn the ropes. College Discovery Tours are conducted by dedicated volunteer guides, enabling supporters to go behind the scenes of this state-of-the-art training facility.

The All-weather Lifeboat Centre, Poole, Dorset

The All-weather Lifeboat Centre (ALC) in Poole is where we make and maintain all of our all-weather lifeboats. The ALC enables us to oversee every stage of the lifeboat design and building process, giving the charity greater control of costs and quality, and ensuring we always have access to the increasingly specialist requirements of world-class lifeboat building. It also means we can efficiently maintain and repair existing lifeboats in

the fleet, guaranteeing optimum lifespans for all our craft, and generating employment, including apprenticeships in marine engineering and boatbuilding. The centre is popular with visitors, and tours of the facility are available.

The Inshore Lifeboat Centre, East Cowes, Isle of Wight

Highly skilled boatbuilders, fitters, electricians and solutionists work on up to 80 inshore lifeboats every year at this facility. All of the charity's inshore lifeboats are built and maintained here, including inflatable B class and D class lifeboats, E class and the lifeguards' inshore rescue boats (IRBs). After the launch of the D class inshore lifeboat in 1963, their manoeuvrability quickly made them a welcome addition, and their use expanded rapidly across the lifeboat station network. This meant that the charity needed a permanent facility to make and maintain its growing fleet of inshore lifeboats. Now the site is also home to the Inshore Lifeboat Visitor and Heritage Centre, opened in 2018 by HRH Princess Anne and a popular tourist attraction on the Isle of Wight.

LEFT: The hull of a Shannon class all-weather lifeboat nears completion at the All-weather Lifeboat Centre.

RIGHT: On the Isle of Wight, RNLI inshore lifeboats are built and maintained at the charity's Inshore Lifeboat Centre.

16

RNLI LIFEGUARDS

Saviours on the beach

In the 200 years since Sir William Hillary established the RNLI, the way that people use the water for fun in the UK and Ireland has changed beyond recognition. In Victorian times, women who wanted to swim in the sea were launched in by big wooden bathing-machines to protect their modesty. Men wore woollen suits and bare chests were not permitted. The sight of people in swimming costumes or shorts on the beach, not to mention surfing or jet-skiing, would have been unimaginable.

But as living standards rose during the 20th century, people began to use the water more and more for pleasure and holiday-making. And by the start of the 21st century it became clear that the RNLI couldn't deliver on Sir William's aim to save lives at sea without also providing lifeguard support on the beaches where it was needed.

RNLI lifeguarding started in 2001 following a successful pilot scheme in the south-west of England. Since then, it has grown into a world-class beach lifeguarding service. Across the UK and Channel Islands, there are now more than 1,500 RNLI lifeguards helping to keep people safe on more than 240 beaches in the summer. They share safety advice, provide first aid to those who need it and save the lives of those who get into trouble in the water. Let's take a closer look at these beach-based lifesavers and how they work.

All about lifeguarding

Lifeguarding is a predominantly summer-based role, and most RNLI lifeguards will tell you that not much beats being able to go to work on the beach and head home later on, knowing you've kept people safe. But being a lifeguard is not about enjoying the sun, sea and sand all day.

It's a saying in lifeguarding circles that a good lifeguard rarely gets wet. That's because most of our lifeguards' work is preventative and based on the idea that when members of the public are as well-informed as possible – about everything from tide times and beach risks to temperatures and weather conditions – the need for actual rescues is much reduced. It also means our lifeguards must still be fit and ready for anything.

The job can be arduous, and it can involve responding in difficult and potentially dangerous conditions. Lifeguards sometimes need to respond to challenging medical emergencies, so they must be able to deliver

casualty care to people young and old. They might also need to take part in prolonged searches.

Being a lifeguard can offer recruits highly desirable and transferable skills that can benefit them as their career develops. Lifeguards can work across a number of different beaches so they have experience applying their skills in a range of settings, from wide-open stretches of sand and busy family spots to craggy coves and surfing meccas. When they're not needed in an actual rescue, lifeguards' duties include patrolling beaches and keeping watch, providing first aid, coordinating with other services on the beach, especially in busy periods, and being a source of local information for everyone who needs them. They develop fast reactions, along with the ability to stay calm under pressure, so they can make split-second decisions, follow instructions and work as part of a team. They need to maintain a high level of fitness in order to be able to do their jobs efficiently and safely.

A key part of an RNLI lifeguard's duty is preventing incidents, through carefully watching the beach, spotting hazards and warning visitors. Lifeguard Mirren McTavish is pictured keeping an eye on the shoreline at Coldingham Bay in the Scottish Borders.

RNLI lifeguards must be able to complete a range of swim tests and be able to run 200m on the beach in under 40 seconds.

Training and qualifying

Just as our lifeboat crews follow a rigorous training programme before they can become fully fledged crew members, so too do our lifeguards. The training programme they go through helps them to build their basic skills – from how to handle and care for equipment on the beach to first aid and casualty care – and they subsequently receive continuous on-the-job training.

Before they join us, our lifeguards also need to meet a set of criteria. First and foremost they need to hold a National Vocational Beach Lifeguard Qualification (NVBLQ) or an international equivalent. To ensure they're physically up to the job they need to pass various physical tests, including an eye test, a 400m pool swim in under 7½ minutes (the first 200m of which must be completed in under 3½ minutes), an underwater pool swim of 25m and a surface swim of 25m, both in 50 seconds or less, and also be able to run 200m on the beach in under 40 seconds. They'll need to be the kind of person who can multitask, get along with people and be proactive. It's only by maintaining this standard of excellence that we can provide the world-class lifeguarding service that we do.

Lifeguard kit

Lifeguards work with some of the most exciting and versatile kit in our range. They need to be able to use a range of equipment, from rescue boards to quad bikes and operate in a range of weather conditions, including blazing heat, strong winds and torrential downpours.

Although they provide a seasonal service, lifeguards need kit that can cope with the changeable weather and sea conditions around our coasts.

When they're not needed in an actual rescue, lifeguard's duties include patrolling beaches, keeping watch and providing first aid.

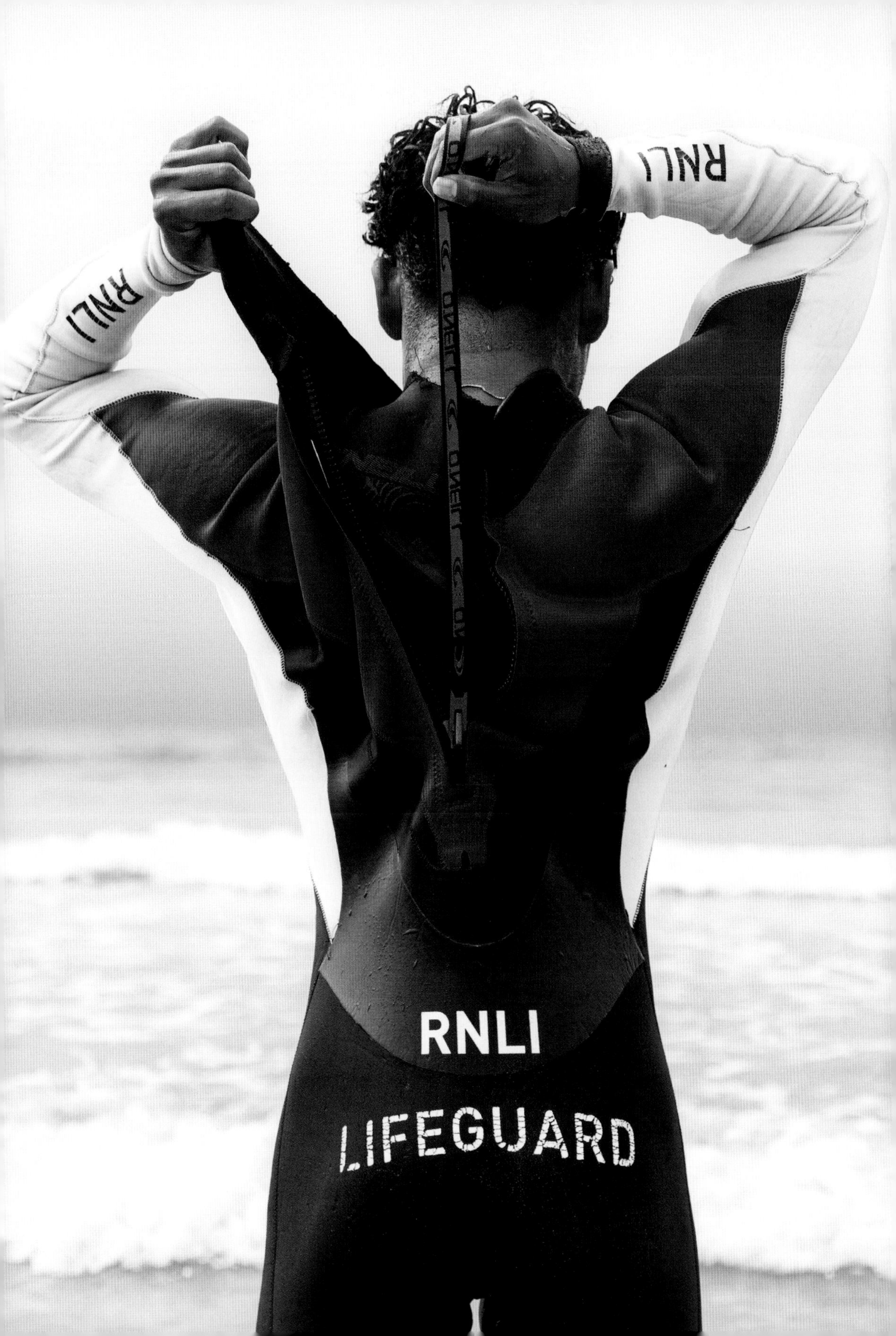
RNLI
RNLI
RNLI
LIFEGUARD

The RNLI's seasonal lifeguard service provides patrols and rescue equipment in beaches around the UK and Channel Islands.

FOCUS ON: JERSEY

In Jersey in the Channel Islands, lifeguard teams are based on beaches at Plémont, El Tico, Watersplash, Le Braye, Grève de Lecq and St Brelade's Bay, with the majority of patrols starting at the end of May and continuing through to September. With so many beaches in one place to coordinate, each with its own unique needs and challenges, preparing for the busy summer season is a huge task. The RNLI has worked with the States of Jersey since 2011 to set up and roll out this lifeguard service every year, recruiting 40 lifeguards, training them and organising delivery of all the equipment they need to do their jobs during the summer months.

RNLI lifeguards Ben, Abigail and Malcolm Greenslade are pictured at Lyme Regis, Dorset in 2023. The three lifeguards are father, son and daughter.

Safety advice from our lifeguards

Whether they are patrolling beaches or visiting inland schools, lifeguards have always played a key role in sharing RNLI safety advice. So what are their top tips?

- Choose a lifeguarded beach if you can.
- Swim between the red and yellow flags.
- Check the weather forecast and tide times, and read local hazard signage to understand local risks.
- Keep a close eye on your family – on the beach and in the water. Don't allow members of your family to swim alone.
- If you fall into the water unexpectedly, FLOAT TO LIVE.
- Tilt your head back with your ears submerged, relax and try to breathe normally and move your hands to help you stay afloat
- In an emergency, dial 999 or 112 and ask for the coastguard.

17

OUTSTANDING ACTS
RNLI medals and how we award them

Every lifesaving act carried out by our lifeboat crew members and lifeguards is remarkable and deserves recognition. But occasionally there are situations in which individuals show exceptional courage and skill in the face of adversity. This is as true today as it was when the RNLI was founded in 1824 – the charity has a long history of awarding medals to those who go above and beyond the call of duty.

Robert 'Scraper' Smith was a lifeboat volunteer for 50 years and from 1909 to 1920 was coxswain at Tynemouth Lifeboat Station, Northumberland. Among other medals, he received the RNLI's Gold and Silver Medals for Gallantry and the Empire Gallantry Medal.

Our medals

Gold

On 4 March 1824, when the RNLI was founded, a number of resolutions were proposed and passed. Resolution Two, proposed by William Wilberforce MP, was that 'medallions or pecuniary awards be given to those who rescue lives in cases of shipwreck'. Later that same year, on 10 July, the first medal was awarded and referred to as a 'Gold Medallion' (read about its first recipient, Captain Charles Fremantle, overleaf). Today a Gold Medal is awarded solely for the most outstanding examples of courage and skill, and it has been compared to the Victoria Cross in its significance and recognition. Only 151 Gold Medals have been awarded in our 200-year history. One Gold Medal has been awarded posthumously, to William Trevelyan Richards, coxswain of the Penlee Lifeboat *Solomon Browne*, which was lost after going to the aid of the coaster *Union Star* on the night of 19 December 1981 (see page 112).

'Today a Gold Medal is awarded solely for the most outstanding examples of courage and skill'

RNLI Medals for Gallantry are not frequently awarded – they are reserved for the most outstanding examples of skill and courage.

Silver

For many years it was common practice mainly to award Silver Medals to coxswains on retirement or resignation from a station after many years of service. The last Silver Medal of this sort was awarded in 1907, not long after motorised lifeboats came into service. They have been also awarded for bravery throughout our history. In 2022 a Silver Medal was awarded to Trearddur Bay Helm Lee Duncan in recognition of his 'leadership, seamanship, and exemplary boat handling in treacherous sea and weather conditions.' This was the first time the helm of an Atlantic 85 lifeboat received a Silver Medal for Gallantry.

Bronze

The first RNLI Bronze Medal for Gallantry was created for Cromer crew members who in 1917 fought fierce conditions for 14 hours to rescue 22 people from the *Pyrin* and 11 people from the wrecked SS *Fernebo*. You can read more about Henry Blogg – Cromer's iconic coxswain on these rescues, who was also awarded a Gold Medal – on page 142. Since then Bronze Medals have been awarded to crews on difficult and courageous call-outs. In 2022 a Bronze Medal was awarded to Port St Mary RNLI Helm Richard Leigh for 'superb boat handling, seamanship, and courage during the rescue of a yacht in rough seas in very demanding circumstances'.

The first medallist

In 1824 Charles Fremantle became the institution's first recipient of a Gold Medal, awarded for his bravery when he swam out to the Swedish brig *Carl Jean*, which was stranded off the coast of Christchurch in Dorset. The boat, bound for Alicante and carrying a precious cargo of salt and wine, had toppled its mast and was in danger of breaking up as the choppy seas slammed into it on all sides.

'In 2022 a Silver Medal was awarded to Trearddur Bay Helm Lee Duncan in recognition of his leadership, seamanship and exemplary boat handling'

Attaching a shore line to his body, Charles swam through the breaking surf to the ship, where he found the terrified crew onboard, refusing to leave their vessel. Charles swam back to shore, where he was said to be 'utterly exhausted and insensible'. The *Carl Jean*'s crew eventually escaped using the ship's broken mast to get to the safety of land.

The full-house medallist

Brian Bevan MBE, former coxswain at Humber Lifeboat Station, is the only crew member in RNLI history to be presented with Bronze, Silver and Gold Medals for Gallantry – and all at the same awards ceremony.

The medals were a result of Brian's bravery during a period of extremely bad weather from December 1978 to February 1979. In seemingly ceaseless strong winds, freezing temperatures and snow, Brian and his crew launched to three rescues near Spurn Point, which saw many of them receive medals for gallantry. But only Brian was awarded all three of the RNLI's medals.

Superintendent Coxswain Brian Bevan was awarded the gold, silver and bronze medals for gallantry for services by Humber lifeboat in some of the worst storms of the past winter. These services were to Revi, Diana V and Savinesti respectively and . . .

. . . the coxswain with his crew, all of whom were awarded the bronze medal for their part in the service to Revi: Crew Member Dennis Bailey, Jnr, Crew Member Peter Jordan, Motor Mechanic Bill Sayers, Superintendent Coxswain Bevan, Second Coxswain Dennis Bailey, Crew Member Sydney Rollinson, Assistant Mechanic Ronald Sayers and Crew Member Michael Storey.
photographs by courtesy of T. M. Carter

This extract from the summer 1979 edition of the *Lifeboat* journal reported an incredible achievement by Humber Coxswain Brian Bevan.

His Bronze came after a 17-hour rescue in blizzards and freezing conditions, helping a Romanian cargo ship carrying 28 people back to safety. The Silver Medal was awarded for his part in rescuing six people, including a 12-year-old girl, from a Dutch coaster being battered in storm-force winds. The Gold Medal was awarded to Brian for his outstanding courage in a rescue on Valentine's Day 1979 when rescuing the crew of the Panamanian motorboat *Revi*. The ship was completely swamped by heavy seas in storm Force 10 conditions 30 miles north of Spurn Point and in danger of sinking. After several attempts, two of *Revi*'s crew were rescued, leaving the captain and mate onboard. After a dozen more attempts, Brian brought the lifeboat alongside and the mate managed to jump onto the lifeboat. The captain was left hanging onto *Revi*'s stern rails waiting to jump. After several more approaches by the lifeboat, *Revi* was swamped and her captain lost.

The youngest medallist

Frederick Carter was only 11 years old when he and his pal Frank Perry, 16, were both awarded Silver Medals in 1890 for a rescue at Weymouth. The contemporary *Lifeboat* journal account says the boys were awarded the medals 'for gallantly saving one of two men whose boat had been capsized in Weymouth Bay in a strong breeze and a heavy surf, on the 26th of May. The two lads, one of whom was sixteen and the other eleven years of age, were in another boat in smooth water, and on observing the casualty, immediately rowed out to the rescue, incurring imminent risk of their boat being either swamped or capsized in the broken water.'

The first lifeguard medallists

In 2003, just two years after the RNLI launched its beach lifeguard service, an Australian man became the RNLI's first lifeguard to receive the Bronze Medal for Gallantry. Sydney-born Rod MacDonald, who was working as a lifeguard at Fistral Beach in Newquay, saved the life of a swimmer who had swum too far from the beach and lost consciousness after being thrown against rocks by strong waves.

With no rescue equipment and wearing only his swimming trunks, Rod clambered down the rocks to a gully and battled the breaking surf to reach the badly injured swimmer. He managed to bring the man to shore and gave him lifesaving first aid until an ambulance arrived. His selflessness undoubtedly saved the man's life, for which Rod was awarded his Bronze Medal.

A few years later in 2006, RNLI Lifeguard Sophie Grant-Crookston was awarded the Bronze Medal for saving a stranded surfer in dangerous seas off Perranporth Beach. Sophie was also the first female lifeguard to receive a Bronze Medal – read more about her rescue on page 59.

Rod MacDonald was the first RNLI lifeguard to receive a Medal for Gallantry.

Other RNLI awards and medals

Special commemorative Platinum Jubilee medals were awarded to 4,500 RNLI volunteers and frontline staff in recognition of the 65,886 lives the charity saved during the 70-year reign of the RNLI Patron, Her Majesty Queen Elizabeth II.

Thanks of the Institution Inscribed on Vellum

Sometimes, if events do not necessarily justify the award of a medal but still deserve recognition, our crew members can be accorded the Thanks of the Institution Inscribed on Vellum or a Framed Letter of Appreciation. Letters of thanks had often been written but the decision was made in 1851 to make the award the Thanks on Vellum. The first Thanks of the Institution Inscribed on Vellum was awarded in February 1852 to Captain Horste, Superintendent of Packets at Holyhead, 'for his promptitude in employing the steam-packet *Anglta* to tow the Holyhead life-boat to the spot where the *Town of Wexford* was wrecked'.

Long Service Badges

Long Service Badges are the RNLI's way of recognising the dedication and commitment of long-serving volunteers. They are awarded to volunteers for reaching landmarks of between 20 and 60 years of service, and recognise the service of volunteers across the many different roles they perform for the RNLI. In 2020, 10 very special people were honoured for more than 60 years of service and 78 people were given awards for over 50 years. Oban RNLI in Argyll and Bute, Scotland, celebrated their achievements with seven of their volunteers reaching medal milestones, totalling 220 years of service to the Scottish lifeboat station.

Lifeguard Supervisor Sam Bailey, Senior Lifeguard Lowri Davies and Lifeguard Macsen Mather received the Alison Saunders Lifeguarding Award for their bravery and skill after saving the lives of a man and his son.

The Alison Saunders Award

The bravery and skill of RNLI lifeguards is recognised each lifeguarding year by the Alison Saunders Lifeguarding Award, sponsored by the retired RNLI Deputy Chair Alison Saunders MBE.

In 2021 the Alison Saunders Lifeguarding Award went to three RNLI lifeguards from Ceredigion after they saved the lives of a man and his 10-year-old son. Working with Cardigan and New Quay RNLI lifeboats, the lifeguards rescued the two kayakers, who had been caught in a strong offshore wind and swept out to sea. The trio showed remarkable courage and selflessness, entering the water with their rescue boards, in the full knowledge that they would be spending a prolonged period of time in the water in cold and difficult conditions.

'I never expected to receive a medal, I didn't join the RNLI to go for medals, but it's an honour for the station and the crew'

A team effort

Ask any RNLI medallist how they did it and they'll more than likely say it was a team effort. This is especially true for lifeboat coxswains because they rarely work in isolation when on a shout, and it is they who most often need to make difficult decisions in a rescue situation and who, ultimately, take responsibility for what happens to the crew.

In 2016 David MacAskill, the coxswain of the Lochinver lifeboat, and his volunteer crew were recognised for their part in saving the lives of four fishermen whose boat was in danger of being swept onto rocks in gale-force winds. They braved 10m seas, thunder, lightning and hail to reach the four people onboard the disabled fishing boat. After battling against the strong winds and waves to attach a tow rope, the lifeboat crew managed to tow it clear of danger.

David was awarded the Bronze Medal for Gallantry for his part in the rescue, while his crew all received Thanks of the Institution Inscribed on Vellum. In an acceptance speech typical of all RNLI coxswains receiving medals for gallantry, David said: 'I never expected to receive a medal. I didn't join the RNLI to go for medals, but it is an honour for the station and the crew as a whole to receive something like this.'

David MacAskill, the coxswain of the Lochinver lifeboat, who was recognised for helping to save the lives of four fishermen.

18

INLAND LIFEBOATS

From Loch Ness to London

Although the majority of the RNLI's 238 lifeboat stations are based at coastal locations, we also provide lifesaving services from some inland waters too. They are relatively new stations in the RNLI's history – the first inland lifeboat station opened in 2001 – and they are found on waterways in Scotland, Northern Ireland and Ireland, and along the Thames in London. As with coastal lifeboat stations, our inland rescue services have developed in response to the demand in the area. Whether it's an increasing number of tourists using the water for pleasure, watersports and angling, or the 24/7 commercial ebb and flow of a busy metropolitan river, our lifeboat crews are ready to rescue.

The first inland station: Enniskillen

When they started operating on Lower Lough Erne, County Fermanagh, Northern Ireland, in May 2001, Eniskillen's lifeboat volunteers became our first inland crew.

Lough Erne is a magnet for anglers, rowers, wakeboarders and other watersports enthusiasts, all of whom have kept the Enniskillen crew very busy. In fact, such is the need for lifesaving support that when it first opened, Enniskillen was the only station to operate four lifeboats: two B class Atlantic 21s and two inshore rescue boats. The Atlantic 21s have since been replaced by an Atlantic 85.

Like their coastal counterparts, Teddington lifeboat volunteers carry pagers and head to the lifeboat station when needed. They serve an eight-mile stretch of the River Thames, from Richmond Half Lock to Molesey Lock.

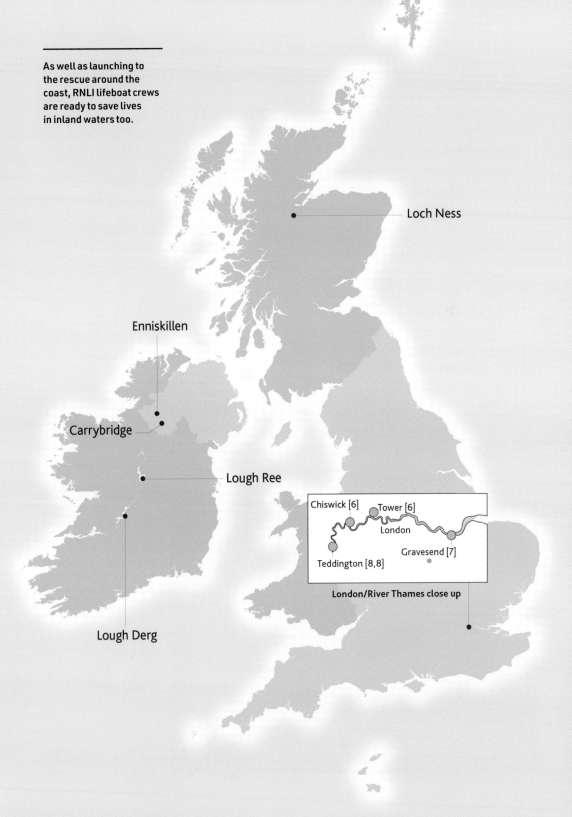

As well as launching to the rescue around the coast, RNLI lifeboat crews are ready to save lives in inland waters too.

Loch Ness

Enniskillen

Carrybridge

Lough Ree

Lough Derg

Chiswick [6]   Tower [6]

London

Teddington [8,8]   Gravesend [7]

London/River Thames close up

Lough Erne is also the only inland waterway where we operate a search and rescue service in two countries. The 26-mile-long Lower Lough Erne, and Upper Lough Erne that flows into it, straddle the border between the UK (Northern Ireland) and the Republic of Ireland. And in 2002, a second inshore lifeboat went into service at Carrybridge on Upper Lough Erne. Lifeboats have been in continuous service at Enniskillen Upper and Lower since 2002. Today, what was once known as Upper is simply known as Carrybridge RNLI.

In 2015 a new station building for Carrybridge was built thanks to kind donors, containing a boathall, mechanics workshop, and changing, training and other facilities. This modern purpose-built lifeboat station is close to the lough, making the launch of its inshore lifeboats as efficient as possible. The station, which also houses a launching tractor and equipment, full crew-changing facilities, a workshop, office and training room, has a ground-source heat pump and solar panels to generate electricity.

River rescuers

Providing a permanent lifeboat service on the Thames became a priority following the tragedy on 20 August 1989, when the party boat *Marchioness* collided with the dredger *Bowbelle* and sank with the loss of 51 lives (see more on page 192). This led to lifeboat crews being established along the Thames at Chiswick, Gravesend, Teddington and Tower.

The area of the Thames served by Gravesend lifeboat crew is home to some of the UK's largest ports with some huge vessels using the river, like this 'Ro-Ro' ship.

The Thames is a particularly cold and fast river, with changing tides and heavy traffic from vessels of all kinds, all of which make it a very dangerous place. That's why our crews at Tower, Chiswick and Gravesend are on duty 24 hours a day, 365 days of the year.

A class of its own

The need for speed is paramount to our work on the Thames, and we designed our E class inshore lifeboat especially for use at Chiswick and Tower Lifeboat Stations. This is the fastest and most nimble boat in our fleet, comfortably reaching top speeds of 40 knots with waterjets that make it easier and quicker to manoeuvre in the fast-flowing water. These lifeboats are kept afloat alongside both stations, for the quickest launch time possible.

Lifesaving on the loch

Loch Ness is Scotland's only inland lifeboat station, providing vital lifesaving support for the thousands of tourists and watersports enthusiasts who flock to the iconic loch every year. The service was established in 2008, and a new boathouse – home to the station's B class Atlantic inshore lifeboat – was built on the loch's north shore after a fundraising campaign in 2015.

Loch Ness lifeboat volunteers pictured afloat shortly after their station opened back in 2008.

Chiswick RNLI's E class
lifeboat crew on exercise.

Although the fabled Loch Ness monster has not yet been spotted by lifeboat volunteers, the crew did respond to an unusual call for help in October 2020, when a Second World War seaplane with four people onboard became stranded on the loch after experiencing engine issues and being unable to take off. The vintage seaplane, a PBY Catalina with a 32-metre wing span, was drifting and exposed in the middle of the loch. Lifeboat volunteers decided the safest way to help would be to tow it to the safety of a mooring buoy. Towing such a large aircraft was no mean feat, and fixing points were few and far between, but the crew eventually managed to fix a tow rope and pulled the seaplane and its grateful crew to the shore station.

Ireland's first inland station: Lough Derg

When it opened in May 2004 at Dromineer on the eastern shore of the lough, Lough Derg, County Tipperary, became Ireland's first inland lifeboat station. Lough Derg is the largest lake on the Shannon River, stretching for 24 miles from Portumna in the north to Killaloe in the south. The busy lough

Loch Derg's B class lifeboat in action.

is popular for sailing, kayaking, fishing and other leisure activities, and the University of Limerick's outdoor activity centre is located by the lake. In June 2013 the Lough Derg lifeboat crew rescued 35 people in a major incident at an international rowing event, the FISA (la Fédération internationale des sociétés d'aviron) World Tour. Despite the high level of experience of those taking part, 18 rowing boats capsized or had to be beached when bad weather closed in on the contest.

Immediate response

Lough Ree is another major lake of the Shannon River and, much like Lough Derg, is popular with fishers, sailors and watersports enthusiasts. The station was established in 2002, but a new state-of-the-art boathouse was built in 2022 on a site donated by the Inland Waterways Association of Ireland. This provides a much-needed training base for the volunteer crew and gives immediate access to the lake for the lifeboat.

'The Lough Derg lifeboat crew rescued 35 people in a major incident at an international rowing event'

19

THE ROYAL CONNECTION

How the Royal Family has worked alongside the RNLI for 200 years

On 20 March 1824, just a few weeks after the National Institution for the Preservation of Life from Shipwreck was founded, the Chairman of the Institution – a Mr Thomas Wilson MP – reported that 'His Grace the Archbishop of Canterbury had communicated to him His Majesty's most Gracious command that the Institution be hereafter authorised to take the name of the "Royal National Institution for the Preservation of Life from Shipwreck".'

The 'Majesty' he spoke of was King George IV, and the 'Gracious command' reported by Mr Wilson signalled the beginning of the Royal Family's longstanding patronage of the RNLI. This prestigious alliance did not come about entirely by chance. Sir William Hillary, the RNLI's founder, had strong Royal connections, having been equerry to King George III's sixth son, Prince Augustus Frederick.

JUNE, 1936.]　　　THE LIFE-BOAT.　　　71

LIFE-BOATMEN IN LONDON.

SALUTING THE KING.

The *Lifeboat* Journal of June 1936 shows the RNLI Gallantry Medallists saluting the charity's Patron, King George V.

The *Lifeboat* Journal of June 1936 described how that year's RNLI Gallantry Medallists travelled to London to collect their awards and saluted the charity's Patron, King George V, as he drove to an Inspection of the Guards. Among the medallists that year were Coxswain Patrick Sliney, of Ballycotton, County Cork; A C Jones, the honorary secretary at Barry Dock, Glamorganshire; Coxswain William Mogridge, of Torbay, Devon; Coxswain Frank Blewett, of Penlee, Cornwall; Coxswain Thomas Sinclair, of Aberdeen; Coxswain James Sim, of Fraserburgh, Aberdeenshire; and Coxswain William Dass, of Longhope, Orkneys.

Patrons of the RNLI: a timeline

1824–1830	King George IV
1830–1837	King William IV
1837–1901	Queen Victoria
1901–1910	King Edward VII
1910–1936	King George V
1911–1953	Queen Mary
1913–1925	Queen Alexandra
1936	King Edward VIII
1937–1952	King George VI
1937–2002	Queen Elizabeth (The Queen Mother)
1952–2022	Queen Elizabeth II

Queen Elizabeth II

Her Late Majesty Queen Elizabeth II, who died in 2022, was our longest-serving Patron and a much-loved member of the RNLI family.

After Queen Elizabeth II came to the throne in 1952, Her Majesty was always there for the RNLI, granting awards for services to lifesaving and sending heartfelt sympathy when we lost crew members to the sea. Her Majesty named lifeboats, opened stations, and brought joy, inspiration and an enormous sense of pride to generations of lifeboat crews and their families.

Early on in Queen Elizabeth II's reign in 1958, Her Majesty and HRH The Prince Philip, Duke of Edinburgh, experienced the unpredictability of all lifeboat crews when Their Royal Highnesses visited Holy Island, Northumberland. RNLI crews from Berwick and North Sunderland launched to proudly escort the Royal Barge, but the coxswain of the North Sunderland lifeboat *Grace Darling* spotted a broken-down motorboat with 14 people onboard in need of help. The lifeboat crew changed course and took the motorboat – *Lady Francis* – under tow to the nearest safe harbour, then returned to complete the Royal Escort.

On 17 July 1972 Queen Elizabeth II became the first reigning Monarch to name a lifeboat. Members of the Royal British Legion had raised £51,000 towards a new Solent class lifeboat to celebrate the Legion's 50th anniversary. Her Majesty was also that charity's Patron, and named the lifeboat *The Royal British Legion Jubilee*. Queen Elizabeth II named four more lifeboats: *The Scout* at Hartlepool in 1977 (see below), *Her Majesty*

In 1977 young Robbie Maiden got to meet HM Queen Elizabeth II during a Royal visit to Hartlepool RNLI as he was the coxswain's son. Robbie went on to become coxswain himself.

The RNLI's Patron for 70 years, HM Queen Elizabeth II opened the RNLI College in 2004.

The Queen at Ramsgate in 1993, *Richard Cox Scott* at Falmouth in 2002 and *Sybil Mullen Glover* at Plymouth in 2003.

Hartlepool's lifeboat-naming ceremony in 1977 was part of HM The Queen's Silver Jubilee. Ten-year-old Robbie Maiden – the coxswain's son at the time – had the honour of meeting the special guest. 'It was a very proud day for me, and one that I still remember,' recalls Robbie, who went on to become coxswain himself. 'The lifeboat crew had arranged for me to have my own RNLI Guernsey jumper and red woolly hat, so I looked like part of the crew. The Queen asked me that day if I wanted to follow in my father's footsteps. The answer was a resounding yes!'

On 28 July 2004, Queen Elizabeth II officially opened the Lifeboat College in Poole, Dorset. Over 200 coxswains and senior helms attended – one each from every RNLI lifeboat station – all in the same place, for the first time ever. Her Majesty and HRH The Prince Philip, Duke of Edinburgh were joined by the RNLI's President, HRH The Duke of Kent, for a tour of the College, including a capsize demonstration in the pool. Their Royal Highnesses then took a short trip around Poole Harbour on a new Severn class lifeboat.

Queen Elizabeth II dedicated 70 years as Patron of the RNLI, engaging with and recognising the efforts of thousands of people. A lot happened in the seven decades of Her Majesty's patronage: RNLI lifeboats launched 329,854 times and saved 65,979 lives. We introduced the lifeguard service

RNLI volunteers were among 200 people from the 2022 Queen's Birthday Honours list to be invited to Her Majesty's State Funeral. Attending on behalf of the charity were fundraiser Lynn Spillett MBE – who was recognised for services to the RNLI in Torbay, Devon; in the seven years when she was chairwoman of fundraising, the branch raised more than £700,000 – and Guy Addington MBE, from Margate in Kent, who saved 13 lives as a crew member and followed in his father's footsteps as lifeboat station manager. Janet Madron BEM officially represented the RNLI – see page 115.

and contactless fundraising, brought jet-propelled lifeboats to the Thames and helped other countries around the world develop their own lifesaving services. None of this would have been possible without the generous and caring support of our Patron throughout that time, Her Majesty Queen Elizabeth II.

HM King Charles III meets RNLI lifesavers during a visit to St Ives, Cornwall.

Bembridge's lifeboat *Queen Victoria* named at an official ceremony by Princess Marie of Battenberg.

What does Royal patronage mean for the RNLI?

For any charitable organisation that relies on donations from the public, the patronage of the Royal Family is a boost to its status, and the regal seal of approval can help attract vital publicity and interest. Whether members of the Royal Family are visiting lifeboat stations, naming new boats or attending other events for the RNLI, the support and enthusiasm of our Royal Patrons always brings with it a huge amount of interest, warmth and generosity from the general public. Now, after 200 years, the Royal Family's unwavering support for the RNLI is stronger than ever. Their continued support and understanding of our lifesaving work are incredibly valued.

'The support and enthusiasm of our Royal Patrons always brings with it a huge amount of interest, warmth and generosity from the general public'

Royal lifeboats

As you'd expect from such a longstanding patronage, there have been more than a few lifeboats named after members of the Royal Family. Queen Victoria had four boats named after her, the first being *ON112 Queen Victoria*, stationed at Bembridge, Isle of Wight, from 1887 to 1902, and the last being part of the relief fleet until 1958. As well as reigning Monarchs, lifeboats have been named after many other Royals, including the Duke of York (at The Lizard, Cornwall, from 1936 to 1961), Princess Alexandra of Kent (at Torbay, Devon, from 1958 and in the relief fleet until 1983) and the Princess of Wales at Barmouth, Gwynedd, from 1982 to 1993.

More recently, in 2011, the Prince and Princess of Wales (Prince William and Catherine Middleton at the time) named a new Atlantic 85 inshore lifeboat as *Hereford Endeavour* on the Welsh island of Anglesey, where Their Royal Highnesses lived. The naming ceremony at Trearddur Bay Lifeboat Station was especially poignant as the Prince, who was a former RAF search and rescue air ambulance pilot, had personally worked with RNLI crews on Anglesey to help save lives at sea.

In 2022 a new state-of–the art Shannon class lifeboat was unveiled at Wells-next-the-Sea, near Sandringham. It was named *Duke of Edinburgh*, to commemorate HRH The Prince Philip, Duke of Edinburgh's long-standing commitment to maritime services. The lifeboat was officially named by HRH The Duke of Kent, the RNLI's President.

The new Shannon class lifeboat, *Duke of Edinburgh*, was officially named by HRH The Duke of Kent.

Presidential support

Long-serving Monarchs are not the only members of of the Royal Family who have dedicated remarkable support to the RNLI. Presidents, vice patrons, heads of fundraising guilds and other roles have been carried out by Royals. HRH The Duke of Kent has served as the RNLI's President since 1969, when the Duke assumed the role from Her Royal Highness Princess Marina, Duchess of Kent. His Royal Highness has shown unwavering support for the RNLI ever since. The Duke has visited almost all of the RNLI lifeboat stations around the coasts of the UK and Ireland and has attended many RNLI events, thanking thousands of crew members, fund-raisers, supporters and staff. In 2023 His Royal Highness opened the new Tower Lifeboat Station (see page 192).

Rescued Royals

In 1881 the Duke and Duchess of Edinburgh became the only two members of the Royal Family to have ever been rescued by a lifeboat. The Duke, who was the son of Queen Victoria and Prince Albert, and the Russian Duchess, the daughter of Emperor Alexander II, were on the way to inspect the lifeboat station at Sidmouth on HMS *Lively*, a Royal Navy frigate. A steamboat was lowered from their ship to take Their Royal Highnesses to the beach, but the swell was rising and the boat very nearly capsized. Fortunately, Sidmouth's lifeboat *Remington* was waiting to be inspected by the very people it now needed to rescue. The lifeboat was quickly launched, and the Duke and Duchess were taken safely to shore.

20

INTERNATIONAL
LIFESAVING
How we help save lives around the world

The RNLI's lifesaving work in the UK and Ireland remains the beating heart of our mission. But as an organisation dedicated to saving the lives of those at sea – and one with such a wealth of lifesaving experience – it is also our duty to share our knowledge with experts in other countries, so that we can make a difference worldwide. Now we're working with countries around the world to help people everywhere benefit from our work.

The hidden tragedy of drowning

Since 2012 the RNLI has been working with international communities and their public health organisations to help with their lifesaving work and development. In particular, we are working to make drowning prevention a priority. The unpublicised tragedy of drowning claims hundreds of thousands of lives every year, especially in parts of Asia and Africa. Here it is a leading killer of children, who do not have the aquatic survival skills and supervision needed to stay safe around the water. Every two minutes of the day someone in the world drowns, and these are preventable deaths.

Through our own preventative and awareness-raising work, the RNLI has proved how simple, low-cost interventions and campaigns can prevent these senseless deaths.

In 2024 the World Health Organization (WHO) estimates that around 235,000 people will drown worldwide. Why are so many people drowning? Over 90% of drownings occur in low- and middle-income countries, where basic water safety education and lifesaving services are minimal. At the same time, people in these countries are often far more exposed to open water, relying on ponds and lakes for daily tasks like washing clothes and bathing.

'The unpublicised tragedy of drowning claims hundreds of thousands of lives every year, especially in parts of Asia and Africa'

Durjoy – shown in a photograph held by his mother – was eight years old when he drowned in a pond in Barishal, Bangladesh. At the last count, an average of 40 children were drowning every day in the country.

Sadly, we know that the real figures for drowning deaths are likely to be far higher. This is because the WHO figures don't include deaths from water-related transport accidents such as ferries sinking or other boat deaths, nor do they include drowning deaths linked to natural disasters such as floods, tsunamis and hurricanes. The number of migrants drowning as they cross open water is also rapidly increasing.

How the RNLI is helping

We believe that anyone can drown, but no one should. So the RNLI is using three main approaches to tackling the global drowning problem: sharing our expertise, with other lifesaving and safety organisations, focusing on a small number of countries to address their drowning problem alongside other organisations, and influencing the decision-makers who can make a global difference.

Sharing our expertise

We have produced free, open-source guides and training materials that help other organisations when it comes to:

The RNLI has worked with communities overseas to develop flood rescue techniques and training.

- **Swim survival and water safety.** We know that equipping children with simple swim and aquatic survival skills makes a huge impact, and have helped set up programmes that train instructors to give children the water safety knowledge and confidence that could save their lives.
- **Setting up a lifeguard service.** Our lifeguarding intervention teams help put lifeguarding patrols in place, including beach profiling, rescue equipment, recruitment and fundraising.
- **Sourcing sustainable lifesaving equipment.** We're working with communities, designers, academics, manufacturers and lifesaving organisations worldwide to develop simple, effective lifesaving kit that can be made and used by the people who need it most – from rescue boards to throw bags.
- **Community first aid training.** For decades the RNLI has trained UK and

Ireland volunteers to care for casualties in all sorts of environments. That expertise has helped to create a manual that can be adapted for use in a variety of environments internationally, empowering people to give basic first aid in their community.

- **Flood safety.** The RNLI has worked with communities to develop throw lines and simple rescue systems they can make and use themselves, as well as working with frontline charity teams so they can safely negotiate floodwaters to deliver aid.
- **Maritime search and rescue:** Many low- and middle-income countries don't have the resources or training to reach people in time when disasters happen at sea. The RNLI works with fellow search and rescue (SAR) teams to share ideas and training. The aim is to help organisations develop an SAR service in their own country, comprising risk assessments and resource planning to training and operations.

Working alongside organisations in other countries

While many of our resources can be shared remotely, some interventions have involved the RNLI teaming up with organisations and communities in their own country to address the drowning epidemic.

Bangladesh

Drowning is a leading killer of children in the country and the biggest killer of children under four years old. Water is everywhere in Bangladesh and the vast majority of land lies less than 10 metres above sea level. The country has 700 rivers and around 5,000 miles of inland waterways. These extensive bodies of water mean children are almost always only a few steps away from danger – research shows that most drownings occur within 20 metres of the home. In Barishal, in Bangladesh's rural south, a number of courageous women are at the heart of a programme that is tackling the area's drowning tragedies. These women, many of them mothers of young children, are stepping forward as community swimming instructors, performing roles once unthinkable in such traditional, conservative communities.

In this region of Bangladesh, many communities are clustered around ponds where people can wash, fish and collect water, but these life-giving ponds also take life away. A survey carried out by Bangladesh's pioneering safety charity, the Centre for Injury Prevention and Research, Bangladesh

The RNLI supports a
Bangladesh-based
water safety project
called Swim Safe.
Developed alongside the
country's own CIPRB
charity, it gives children
aquatic survival skills in
their own communities.

(CIPRB), found that 40 children were drowning a day, with the majority of young lives lost in inland ponds. Because their parents are working and doing essential chores, these children often have no adult supervision, no swimming skills and no knowledge of how to be safe around water.

But that is changing thanks to the Swim Safe programme, created in partnership with the CIPRB and funded by supportive organisations such as The Lifeboat Fund, the Isle of Man Government and the Princess Charlene of Monaco Foundation. Swimming instructors receive a week of intensive training before starting regular sessions with the children. This all leads towards an assessment where each child must show they can swim 25m and float for 30 seconds. They also learn how to help others in difficulty without putting themselves in danger.

Tanzania

In Lake Victoria, Tanzania, drowning exceeds each of the national death rates for HIV, tuberculosis and malaria. In 2018, RNLI-funded research showed that the figures for drownings were severely underreported. A staggering 86 people drowned from just a handful of villages alone. It's one of the most dangerous stretches of water in the world in terms of the number of fatalities.

Since then, the RNLI has started to work with EMEDO (Environmental Management and Economic Development Organization), a local development group which works to empower rural communities for improved livelihoods. Working with the RNLI, EMEDO have trialled interventions with the Tanzanian fishing communities – buoyancy aids, weather reporting by text messaging, fishing safety plans at each location and water safety education in schools.

As part of the project, fisher Jing'oi Masatu was given a lifejacket by the boat owner who had attended a water safety session in Kome. He said: 'We were going fishing when we crashed the boat and I found myself in the water. The other fishermen didn't realise I was in the water, but later on they came back for me. I was floating because of the lifejacket and they rescued me. Without this lifejacket I would have died because I don't know how to swim.'

Saving your own child's life

For one woman, the RNLI-supported safety training she received meant she was actually able to save her own child's life. Jhorna Begum is the mother of two boys, Robiul and Yasin. The boys were at home while she was at work one morning, and Yasin, who was four years old at the time, went missing. Robiul raised the alarm and, after a frantic search, Yasin's shoe was spotted in a nearby pond. Jhorna's husband jumped in and pulled the unconscious child onto land. Thankfully, Jhorna was able to recall the vital training she had received as part of her involvement with the CIPRB and Swim Safe. She said: 'I checked but there was no sign of breathing. So I laid Yasin down and breathed through his mouth. After three attempts at this, Yasin moved slightly. When I kept doing the same thing, he regained consciousness. I saved my child. The only reason I could save him was because of my training. So I say thank you to everyone who helped me learn.'

Jhorna Begum saved her son's life using the training she received in an RNLI-supported project.

Twelve candidates from nine countries are pictured taking part in the RNLI's Leaders in Lifesaving course. The course aims to increase knowledge and skills in leadership, drowning prevention and technical lifesaving skills. The delegates arrive ready to learn and share their drowning prevention experience, and always leave with invaluable lifesaving knowledge.

Getting drowning onto the global agenda

Our international work has begun to influence the policy and practice of national governments, non-governmental organisations and the United Nations. With the RNLI's support, several governments came together in New York in 2018 to form a Group of Friends on Drowning Prevention. With the RNLI acting as secretariat, the Group of Friends on Drowning Prevention supported events to raise awareness of drowning prevention with other governments and worked to secure a first-ever UN resolution. The governments of Bangladesh and Ireland took a lead in this effort and, in April 2021, the UN General Assembly adopted a historic resolution on Global Drowning Prevention. This resolution establishes drowning as an important international issue, recognised by all 193 Member States of the UN, and sets out the actions that every country should take to prevent drowning. The resolution also established an annual World Drowning Prevention Day to be marked on 25 July each year.

In Lake Victoria, Tanzania, drowning exceeds each of the national death rates for HIV, tuberculosis and malaria.

How does the RNLI fund its international work?

As a charity, the RNLI has benefited from donations from individuals, trusts, foundations and other donors who specifically want to fund our international activity, including dedicated international development funding to date from the UK, Irish and Isle of Man governments. Our international work also has access to RNLI general funds in the same way as our domestic activity.

On the world's longest natural sea beach at Cox's Bazar in Bangladesh, a lifeguard patrols the shore. Funded by a variety of organisations and set up with the country's own safety charity CIPRB, the lifeguards and their trainers developed their skills in partnership with the RNLI.

DISCOVER OUR HISTORY

Get more sights and sounds from our history at RNLI.org/OurHistory

1824
The Royal National Institution for the Preservation of Life from Shipwreck is founded by Sir William Hillary. The Institution's first Gold Medal is awarded to Charles Fremantle for his efforts to save the crew of a wrecked brigantine off the coast of Hampshire.

1838
Grace Darling and her father, a lighthouse keeper, rescue survivors from the *Forfarshire*, wrecked on the Farne Islands. The Darlings are awarded RNLI Silver Medals and become national celebrities, focusing public attention on saving lives at sea.

1854
The charity's name is changed to the Royal National Lifeboat Institution (RNLI). Cork lifejackets are issued to crew members for the first time.

1861
Whitby lifeboat capsizes and 12 out of 13 crew drown. The sole survivor, Henry Freeman, is the only one wearing a lifejacket.

1891
The first RNLI street collection is held in Manchester.

1914
As lifeboatmen are called away to the First World War, the average age of crews increases to over 50. During the war years (1914–18), lifeboats are launched 1,808 times and their crews save 5,332 lives.

1939
Young lifeboat volunteers are again called away to war. By the end of the Second World War in 1945, RNLI crews have saved 6,376 lives.

1940
Nineteen RNLI lifeboats help evacuate Allied troops from Dunkirk.

1941
Cromer Coxswain Henry Blogg is awarded his third RNLI Gold Medal after going to the aid of a stranded convoy. He remains the RNLI's most decorated crew member.

1963
Inflatable lifeboats are introduced to the RNLI fleet to help deal with the growing number of incidents close to shore. Today's D class lifeboats are direct descendants.

1969

Elizabeth Hostvedt of Atlantic College becomes the first woman qualified to command a lifeboat.

1981

The eight crew of the Penlee lifeboat *Solomon Browne* are lost as they attempt to save those onboard the coaster *Union Star*.

1995

The RNLI's Sea Safety campaign is launched, with the aim of preventing seagoers from getting into trouble in the first place.

2001

RNLI lifeguards begin patrolling beaches in south-west England. The service is expanded to other areas in the following years. The first inland lifeboat station is established at Enniskillen.

2002

Four lifeboat stations are established along the River Thames, following an inquiry into the 1989 *Marchioness* disaster.

2003

Rod MacDonald becomes the first RNLI lifeguard to be awarded an RNLI Medal for Gallantry, for saving a swimmer off Fistral Beach, Newquay.

2005

Helm Aileen Jones becomes the first female crew member to be awarded an RNLI Medal for Gallantry.

2012

The RNLI's International programme begins, working with partners worldwide to understand and tackle the global drowning epidemic.

2015

The All-weather Lifeboat Centre opens in Poole. The RNLI now builds and maintains its own all-weather lifeboats.

2021

The first World Drowning Prevention Day runs on 25 July, after UN member states show their commitment to water safety by adopting the UN's first resolution on drowning prevention.

2024

It's the RNLI's 200th anniversary. With you by our side, we commemorate our past, celebrate modern-day lifesavers and inspire a new generation.

RNLI MEMORIAL LIST

* Pre-RNLI
** Private lifeboat or pre-RNLI at this location

STATION NAME	NAME	YEAR	STATION NAME	NAME	YEAR
Aberdovey	O Owen	1862	Ballywalter	R Boyd	1868
Aberdovey	J Price	1898	Banff	J McDonald	1847
Aberystwyth	J James	1877	Barra Island	J MacNeil	1942
Ackergill	R Bain	1876	Barry Dock	F Swarts	1965
Ackergill	J Cormack	1876	Berwick-upon-Tweed	T Elliott	1877
Ackergill	W Gunn	1876	Blackpool	J Rimmer	1880
Ackergill	J Sutherland	1876	Blyth	T Brown	1810 *
Aldeburgh	T Cable	1859	Blyth	J Dobie	1810 *
Aldeburgh	PF Green	1859	Blyth	J Hall	1810 *
Aldeburgh	J Pearce	1859	Blyth	W Hunter	1810 *
Aldeburgh	E Butcher	1893	Blyth	M Jefferson	1810 *
Aldeburgh	J Butcher	1899	Blyth	G Lee	1810 *
Aldeburgh	C Crisp	1899	Blyth	J Morgan	1810 *
Aldeburgh	H Downing	1899	Blyth	W Oliver	1810 *
Aldeburgh	A Easter	1899	Blyth	J Partis	1810 *
Aldeburgh	T Morris	1899	Blyth	J Robinson	1810 *
Aldeburgh	JM Ward	1899	Blyth	H Short	1810 *
Aldeburgh	W Ward	1899	Blyth	D Stewart	1810 *
Appledore	S Blackmore	1833 **	Blyth	W Todd	1810 *
Appledore	J Peake	1833 **	Blyth	T Turnbull	1810 *
Appledore	B Pile	1833 **	Blyth	J Walker	1810 *
Appledore	D Johns	1868	Blyth	R Burn	1841 **
Arbroath	P Swankie	1911	Blyth	P Bushell	1841 **
Arbroath	T Adams	1953	Blyth	D Dawson	1841 **
Arbroath	D Bruce	1953	Blyth	H Debord	1841 **
Arbroath	C Cargill	1953	Blyth	W Dixon	1841 **
Arbroath	D Cargill	1953	Blyth	JT Heppell	1841 **
Arbroath	H Swankie	1953	Blyth	G Heron	1841 **
Arbroath	W Swankie (Jnr)	1953	Blyth	J Hudson	1841 **
Ardrossan	W Breckenridge	1880	Blyth	J White	1841 **
Ardrossan	W Grier	1880	Blyth	E Wood	1841 **
Ardrossan	A McEwan	1880	Blyth	MA Fairhurst	1898
Arklow	J Dunne	1902	Boulmer	J Stanton	1912
Arranmore	H McGill	1930	Brancaster	H Southland	1890
Atherfield	J Heal	1848	Bridlington	R Atkin	1871 **
Atherfield	W Wearn	1848	Bridlington	J Clappison	1871 **
Bacton	J Haylett	1880	Bridlington	W Cobb	1871 **
Bacton	J Stageman	1880	Bridlington	R Pickering	1871 **
Ballycotton	W Harding	1911	Bridlington	D Purdon	1871 **

STATION NAME	NAME	YEAR	STATION NAME	NAME	YEAR
Bridlington	J Watson	1871 **	Caister	W Wilson	1901
Bridlington	C Brown	1898 **	Caister	J Haylett	1919
Bridlington	R Carr	1915	Caister (Independent)	RW Read	1991 **
Bridlington	RP Redhead	1952	Camber	T Bolton	1838
Bridlington	J Shippey	1964	Camber	R Connors	1838
Brighstone Grange	T Cotton	1888	Camber	I Falling	1838
Brighstone Grange	M Munt	1888	Camber	J Scammel	1838
Brighton	J Laker	1860	Cardigan	D Richards	1867
Broadstairs	SJ Pettit	1901	Carnarvon	E Hughes	1824
Broadstairs	TH Wales	1907	Carnarvon	W Hughes	1824
Brooke	McLeod	1865	Carnarvon	Hughes	1824
Brooke	R Cooper	1888	Carnarvon	Hughes	1824
Broughty Ferry	DG Anderson	1959	Carnarvon	O Owens	1824
Broughty Ferry	J Ferrier	1959	Cemlyn	J Williams	1908
Broughty Ferry	AS Gall	1959	Clacton-on-Sea	T Cattermole	1884
Broughty Ferry	R Grant	1959	Clacton-on-Sea	J Cross	1884
Broughty Ferry	J Grieve	1959	Clacton-on-Sea	B Addis	1888
Broughty Ferry	JJ Grieve	1959	Clacton-on-Sea	F Castle	1943
Broughty Ferry	GB Smith	1959	Clogher Head	HW Pullan	1902
Broughty Ferry	G Watson	1959	Clogher Head	J Crosby	1858
Buddon Ness	Knight	1848	Clogher Head	G Hughes	1858
Bude	N Bradden	1844	Clogher Head	JJ Kelly	1858
Bude	W Skitch	1844	Clogher Head	J Murphy	1858
Bude	J Maynard	1877	Clovelly	J Dunn	1902
Caister	J Burton	1885	Courtown	R Flinn	1868
Caister	F Haylett	1885	Courtown	SH Jenkins	1868
Caister	J Haylett	1885	Courtown	J Randall	1868
Caister	G Hodds	1885	Courtown	W Smith	1868
Caister	J King	1885	Cresswell	HJ Brown	1899
Caister	W Knowles	1885	Cromer	J Sharp	1918
Caister	J Riches	1885	Cromer	EW Allen	1941
Caister	J Sutton	1885	Cullercoats	JL Abel	1939
Caister	S Brown	1897	Cullercoats	JR Armstrong	1939
Caister	C Brown	1901	Cullercoats	KL Biggar	1939
Caister	W Brown	1901	Cullercoats	Lt Cdr LER Blakeney-Booth RN	1939
Caister	C George	1901	Cullercoats	G Brunton	1939
Caister	AW Haylett	1901	Cullercoats	JH Scott	1939
Caister	J Haylett (Jnr)	1901	Cullercoats	T Stewart	1950
Caister	G King	1901	Donna Nook	J Phillips	1884
Caister	H Knights	1901	Donna Nook	D Brooks	1886
Caister	J Smith	1901	Donna Nook	A Richards	1886

STATION NAME	NAME	YEAR	STATION NAME	NAME	YEAR
Douglas	T Freet	1877	Dunbar	W Lucas	1845
Douglas	J Campbell	1881	Dunbar	W Miller	1845
Douglas	T Clucas	1881	Dunbar	Lt S Wylde RN	1845
Douglas	G Elliot	1881	Dunbar	R Clements	1877
Douglas	T Kelly	1881	Dunbar	R Harkis	1877
Douglas	W Gordon	1891	Dungarvon	T Crawford	1852
Douglas	JD Hay	1893	Dungarvon	Capt M Duggan	1852
Dover	A Nash	1903	Dungarvon	L Lenihan	1852
Dun Laoghaire	J Archbold	1821	Dungarvon	J Maher	1852
Dun Laoghaire	H Byrne	1821	Dungarvon	T McNamara	1852
Dun Laoghaire	T Fitzsimons	1821	Dungarvon	M Mulcahy	1852
Dun Laoghaire	T Grimes	1821	Dungarvon	M Raher	1852
Dun Laoghaire	Capt JM Boyd RN	1861	Dungarvon	J Whelan	1852
Dun Laoghaire	J Curry	1861	Dungarvon	M Hogan	1895
Dun Laoghaire	A Forsyth	1861	Dungeness	T Fletcher	1852
Dun Laoghaire	J Johnson	1861	Dungeness	P Light	1852
Dun Laoghaire	T Murphy	1861	Dungeness	T Noble	1852
Dun Laoghaire	J Russell	1861	Dungeness	Unknown	1852
Dun Laoghaire	B Mundone	1876	Dungeness	G Hamlin	1889
Dun Laoghaire	T White	1876	Dungeness	D Nicolls	1891
Dun Laoghaire	P Hammond	1892	Dungeness	H Reeves	1891
Dun Laoghaire	J Baker	1895	Dungeness	JS Jarrett	1893
Dun Laoghaire	J Bartley	1895	Dungeness	G Campbell	1898
Dun Laoghaire	E Crowe	1895	Dunmore East	P Bouchier	1893
Dun Laoghaire	T Dunphy	1895	Eastbourne	H Hendy	1926
Dun Laoghaire	W Dunphy	1895	Exmouth	FH Horne	1905
Dun Laoghaire	F McDonald	1895	Exmouth	HC Squire	1907
Dun Laoghaire	E Murphy	1895	Exmouth	PS Gifford	1953
Dun Laoghaire	P Power	1895	Exmouth	W Carder	1956
Dun Laoghaire	J Ryan	1895	Falmouth	T Pratt	1941
Dun Laoghaire	F Saunders	1895	Fethard	W Banville	1914
Dun Laoghaire	G Saunders	1895	Fethard	C Bird	1914
Dun Laoghaire	E Shannon	1895	Fethard	W Bird	1914
Dun Laoghaire	H Underhill	1895	Fethard	P Cullen	1914
Dun Laoghaire	A Williams	1895	Fethard	M Handrick	1914
Dun Laoghaire	H Williams	1895	Fethard	T Handrick	1914
Dun Laoghaire	P Crowe	1906	Fethard	J Morrissey	1914
Dunbar	B Wilson	1810 *	Fethard	P Roche	1914
Dunbar	W Clements	1845	Fethard	P Stafford	1914
Dunbar	D Davey	1845	Filey	JW Willis	1930
Dunbar	P Davey	1845	Filey	RF Appleby	1974

STATION NAME	NAME	YEAR	STATION NAME	NAME	YEAR
Fishguard	C Grinder	1866	Gorleston	T Morley	1867 **
Fishguard	TM Neal	1944	Gorleston	W Moss	1867 **
Flamborough	M Chadwick	1909	Gorleston	J Sheen	1867 **
Flamborough	G Gibbon	1909	Gorleston	N Spurgeon	1867 **
Flamborough	TL Major	1909	Gorleston	A George	1888 **
Fleetwood	J Abram	1890	Gorleston	S George	1888 **
Fleetwood	G Greenall	1890	Gorleston	W Whiley	1888 **
Fleetwood	W Wright	1945	Gorleston	A Woods	1888 **
Flint	WE Towers	2001	Gorleston	J Adams	1894
Formby	J Brooks	1836 **	Great Yarmouth	W Brown	1824
Formby	R Formby	1836 **	Great Yarmouth	J Church	1824
Formby	W Rimmer	1836 **	Great Yarmouth	J Page	1824
Formby	T Swift	1836 **	Great Yarmouth	S Woods	1824
Formby	J Walker	1836 **	Great Yarmouth	W Woods	1824
Fraserburgh	A Farquhar	1919	Great Yarmouth	G Barney	1845
Fraserburgh	A Noble	1919	Great Yarmouth	J Boulton	1845
Fraserburgh	J Buchan	1953	Great Yarmouth	J George	1845
Fraserburgh	J Crawford	1953	Great Yarmouth	G Hilling	1845
Fraserburgh	G Duthie	1953	Great Yarmouth	J Shreeve	1845
Fraserburgh	J Noble	1953	Great Yarmouth	W Warner	1845
Fraserburgh	A Ritchie	1953	Great Yarmouth	A Wetherall	1845
Fraserburgh	C Tait	1953	Great Yarmouth	C Beckett	1881
Fraserburgh	J Buchan	1970	Great Yarmouth	J Ditcham	1881
Fraserburgh	JRS Buchan	1970	Great Yarmouth	W Green	1881
Fraserburgh	W Hadden	1970	Great Yarmouth	H Masterson	1881
Fraserburgh	F Kirkness	1970	Great Yarmouth	J Sherwood	1881
Fraserburgh	J Stephen	1970	Great Yarmouth	R Symonds	1881
Gorleston	W Dawkins	1866 **	Greystones	J Doyle	1892
Gorleston	J Fleming	1866 **	Grimsby	C Barr	1893
Gorleston	B Harris	1866 **	Grimsby	R Little	1916
Gorleston	W Manthorpe	1866 **	Hartlepool	T Kennedy	1959
Gorleston	A Newson	1866 **	Harwich	W Wink	1881
Gorleston	C Parker	1866 **	Harwich	G Wyatt	1869
Gorleston	R Spillings	1866 **	Hayle	JP Warren	1883
Gorleston	E Welton	1866 **	Hilbre Island	E Lilley	1899
Gorleston	C Whiley	1866 **	Holyhead	W Hughes	1865
Gorleston	C Woods	1866 **	Holyhead	R Jones	1892
Gorleston	E Woods (Snr)	1866 **	Holyhead	J Owen	1901
Gorleston	J Woods (Jnr)	1866 **	Holyhead	T Owen	1901
Gorleston	C Hannent	1867 **	Holyhead	TJ Michael	1920
Gorleston	J Leggett	1867 **	Howth	P Rourke	1949

STATION NAME	NAME	YEAR	STATION NAME	NAME	YEAR
Hoylake	H Bird	1810 *	Liverpool	J Mason	1865 **
Hoylake	H Bird	1810 *	Liverpool	A Miller	1865 **
Hoylake	J Bird	1810 *	Liverpool	B Murphy	1865 **
Hoylake	J Bird	1810 *	Liverpool	J Boyle	1875 **
Hoylake	J Hughes	1810 *	Liverpool	R Moore	1875 **
Hoylake	R Hughes	1810 *	Liverpool	J Yates	1875 **
Hoylake	T Hughes	1810 *	Liverpool	D Morgan	1892 **
Hoylake	Unknown	1810 *	Liverpool	E Rodriguez	1892 **
Hoylake	Jl Roberts	1906	Liverpool	W Ruffler	1892 **
Hythe	C Fagg	1891	Llanddwyn	W Owen	1847 **
Ilfracombe	F Souch	1895	Llandudno	E Jones	1887
Ilfracombe	R Souch	1895	Llandudno	R Williams	1890
Irish Air Corps	Capt M Baker	1999	Llandudno	A Whalley	1892
Irish Air Corps	Cpl N Byrne	1999	Llandudno	J Williams	1908
Irish Air Corps	Sgt P Mooney	1999	Longhope	J Johnston	1969
Irish Air Corps	Capt D O'Faherty	1999	Longhope	R Johnston	1969
Irish Naval Service	LS M Quinn DSM	1990	Longhope	RR Johnston	1969
Islay	A McNeill	1953	Longhope	D Kirkpatrick BEM	1969
Islay	J MacTaggart	1953	Longhope	DR Kirkpatrick	1969
Johnshaven	J McBay	1920	Longhope	JT Kirkpatrick	1969
Kessingland	T Tripp	1875	Longhope	ES McFadyen	1969
Kilmore Quay	FM Sinnott	1977	Longhope	J Swanson	1969
Kingsdowne	F Arnold	1902	Lyme Regis	H Cox	1852
Kirkcudbright	P McGinn	1864	Lyme Regis	T Black	1852
Lerwick	W Deacon	1997	Lyme Regis	H Hearne	1852
Liverpool	J Brown	1854 **	Lyme Regis	W Harvey	1852
Liverpool	Burdick	1854 **	Lyme Regis	J Martin	1854
Liverpool	J Davies (Snr)	1854 **	Lyme Regis	J Gerrard	1861
Liverpool	J Davies (Jnr)	1854 **	Lyme Regis	R Jefford	1969
Liverpool	J Gee	1854 **	Lytham	G Cookson	1852 **
Liverpool	S Griffiths	1854 **	Lytham	J Davies	1852 **
Liverpool	T Hayes	1854 **	Lytham	J Gillett	1852 **
Liverpool	Ogden	1854 **	Lytham	T Gillett	1852 **
Liverpool	H Pearson	1854 **	Lytham	T Hardman	1852 **
Liverpool	W Roberts	1854 **	Lytham	W Swann	1852 **
Liverpool	Shaw	1854 **	Lytham	J Whiteside	1852 **
Liverpool	H Wilson	1854 **	Lytham	J Winders	1852 **
Liverpool	R Clark	1865 **	Lytham	J Parkinson	1886
Liverpool	H Green	1865 **	Mallaig	P Morrison	2001
Liverpool	J Martindale	1865 **	Margate	F Bath	1857
Liverpool	P Martindale	1865 **	Margate	A Busbridge	1857

STATION NAME	NAME	YEAR	STATION NAME	NAME	YEAR
Margate	J Emptage	1857	Newhaven	J Richards	1910
Margate	W Emptage	1857	Newhaven	R Payne	1931
Margate	C Fuller	1857	Newhaven	BJ Clark	1943
Margate	H Paramor	1857	Newquay	H Storey	1908
Margate	G Smith	1857	Padstow	Unknown	1814 *
Margate	J Smith	1857	Padstow	Unknown	1814 *
Margate	I Solly	1857	Padstow	Unknown	1814 *
Margate	HR Brockman	1897 **	Padstow	Unknown	1814 *
Margate	RE Cook	1897 **	Padstow	J Dymond	1816 *
Margate	WP Cook (Snr)	1897 **	Padstow	S Gay	1816 *
Margate	WP Cook (Jnr)	1897 **	Padstow	J Russell	1816 *
Margate	ER Crunden	1897 **	Padstow	J Chapman	1826
Margate	JB Dyke	1897 **	Padstow	H Trebilcock	1826
Margate	WR Gill	1897 **	Padstow	J Trebilcock	1826
Margate	GRW Ladd	1897 **	Padstow	D Shea	1867
Margate	CE Troughton	1897 **	Padstow	W Intross	1867
Margate	T Ashley	1904	Padstow	T Varco	1867
Margate	JJ Jones	1906 **	Padstow	M Crannell	1867
Margate	B Frost	1949	Padstow	A Truscott	1867
Minehead	WP Slade	1911	Padstow	JW Bate	1900
Minehead	T Escott	1941	Padstow	S East	1900
Minehead	J Slade	1941	Padstow	D Grubb	1900
Moelfre	W Roberts	1927	Padstow	J Grubb	1900
Montrose	A Paton	1872	Padstow	E Kane	1900
New Brighton	C Finlay	1883	Padstow	JS Martin	1900
New Brighton	A Dodd	1905	Padstow	JB Old	1900
New Brighton	J Jones	1905	Padstow	J Stephens	1900
New Brighton	G Cross	1922	Padstow	TB Cowl	1935
New Brighton	WJ Liversage	1923	Palling	R Amis	1910
New Brighton	H Harrison	1925	Penarth	J F Jackson	1891
New Brighton	J Stonall	1938	Penarth	Redmond	1891
New Brighton	FK Neilson	1962	Penlee	J Pentreath	1961
New Romney	T Brice	1874	Penlee	JR Blewett	1981
New Romney	S Hart	1891	Penlee	N Brockman	1981
New Romney	W Ryan	1891	Penlee	CT Greenhaugh	1981
New Romney	J Sullivan	1891	Penlee	JS Madron	1981
Newbiggin	C Storey	1972	Penlee	WT Richards	1981
Newburgh	J Walker	1942	Penlee	K Smith	1981
Newburgh	GB Whyte	1942	Penlee	BR Torrie	1981
Newcastle	P Goolaghan	1837	Penlee	GL Wallis	1981
Newcastle	G Starkey	1837	Peterhead	J Geddes	1914

STATION NAME	NAME	YEAR	STATION NAME	NAME	YEAR
Peterhead	TA Geddes	1914	Rhosneigr	R Eaton	1941
Peterhead	DM Strachan	1914	Rhosneigr	LA Ford	1941
Peterhead	C Cameron	1929	Rhosneigr	E Jones	1941
Point of Ayr	R Beck	1857 **	Rhosneigr	AW Moger	1941
Point of Ayr	J Bleddyn	1857 **	Rhosneigr	AJ Owen	1941
Point of Ayr	D Davies	1857 **	Rhosneigr	RK Simons	1941
Point of Ayr	J Davies	1857 **	Rhosneigr	CH Thornton	1941
Point of Ayr	R Davies	1857 **	Rhosneigr	PT Whysall	1941
Point of Ayr	J Ellis	1857 **	Rhosneigr	S Wilkins	1941
Point of Ayr	T Owen	1857 **	Rhyl	J Edwards	1853
Point of Ayr	E Phillips	1857 **	Rhyl	J Evans	1853
Point of Ayr	E Roberts	1857 **	Rhyl	D George	1853
Point of Ayr	R Roberts	1857 **	Rhyl	P Jones	1853
Point of Ayr	T Roberts	1857 **	Rhyl	T Jones	1853
Point of Ayr	J Sherlock	1857 **	Rhyl	W Parry	1853
Point of Ayr	R Williams	1857 **	Robin Hood's Bay	R Avery	1843
Poole	J Hughes	1884	Robin Hood's Bay	E Gillons	1843
Port Erroll	C Summers	1913	Robin Hood's Bay	Lt J Lingard RN	1843
Port Eynon	W Eynon	1916	Robin Hood's Bay	W Pond	1843
Port Eynon	W Gibbs	1916	Robin Hood's Bay	C Trueman	1843
Port Eynon	G Harry	1916	Robin Hood's Bay	W Turner	1843
Port St Mary	E Kneen	1927	Runswick	R Patton	1934
Port St Mary	J Evans	1937	Ryde	F Haynes	1907
Portrush	G Grills	1889	Ryde	H Heward	1907
Portrush	J McAlister	1889	Rye Harbour	L Clark	1928
Portrush	W McNeill	1889	Rye Harbour	W Clark	1928
Ramsey	EB Kinnin	1958	Rye Harbour	AE Cutting	1928
Ramsgate	W White	1873	Rye Harbour	H Cutting	1928
Redcar	W Guy	1836	Rye Harbour	RR Cutting	1928
Redcar	E Picknett	1901	Rye Harbour	A Downey	1928
Redcar	J Picknett	1901	Rye Harbour	MJ Downey	1928
Redcar	R Picknett	1901	Rye Harbour	H Head	1928
Redcar	Mrs M Emmans	1921	Rye Harbour	J Head	1928
Rhoscolyn	E Hughes	1920	Rye Harbour	J Head	1928
Rhoscolyn	R Hughes	1920	Rye Harbour	W Igglesden	1928
Rhoscolyn	O Jones	1920	Rye Harbour	CFD Pope	1928
Rhoscolyn	O Owens	1920	Rye Harbour	LA Pope	1928
Rhoscolyn	W Thomas	1920	Rye Harbour	RH Pope	1928
Rhosneigr	W Roberts	1895	Rye Harbour	AE Smith	1928
Rhosneigr	GC Arthur	1941	Rye Harbour	C Southerden	1928
Rhosneigr	DW Bannister	1941	Rye Harbour	J Stonham	1928

STATION NAME	NAME	YEAR	STATION NAME	NAME	YEAR
St Agnes	WT Hicks	1907	Scarborough	J Allen	1836 **
St Andrews	G Sharp	1898	Scarborough	T Boyes	1836 **
St Andrews	P Flannagan	1932	Scarborough	J Clayburn	1836 **
St Annes	J Bonney	1886	Scarborough	T Cross	1836 **
St Annes	T Bonney	1886	Scarborough	JO Dale	1836 **
St Annes	J Dobson	1886	Scarborough	J Day	1836 **
St Annes	R Fisher	1886	Scarborough	R Marchman	1836 **
St Annes	J Harrison	1886	Scarborough	J Maw	1836 **
St Annes	O Hodson	1886	Scarborough	T Walker	1836 **
St Annes	J Johnson	1886	Scarborough	J Waugh	1836 **
St Annes	W Johnson	1886	Scarborough	Lord C Beauclerk	1861
St Annes	N Parkinson	1886	Scarborough	T Brewster	1861
St Annes	T Parkinson	1886	Scarborough	J Burton	1861
St Annes	C Tims	1886	Scarborough	J Iles	1861
St Annes	R Tims	1886	Scarborough	W Tindall	1861
St Annes	J Wignall	1886	Scarborough	F Dalton	1951
St Davids	J Price	1910	Scarborough	F Bayes	1954
St Davids	H Rowlands	1910	Scarborough	JH Cammish	1954
St Davids	J Stephens	1910	Scarborough	JN Sheader	1954
St Davids	IM Bateman	1956	Seaham	A Brown	1962
St Ives	MS Barber	1939	Seaham	A L Brown	1962
St Ives	WB Barber	1939	Seaham	J Farrington	1962
St Ives	E Bassett	1939	Seaham	F Gippert	1962
St Ives	JB Cocking	1939	Seaham	JT Miller	1962
St Ives	T Cocking	1939	Seaton Carew	G Cowell	1867
St Ives	RQ Stevens	1939	Shoreham Harbour	R Brazier	1874
St Ives	J Thomas	1939	Sidmouth (Independent)	A Squance	1989
St Peter Port	HF Hobbs	1940	Silloth	J Bell	1956
Salcombe	JA Canham	1916	Silloth	S Graham	1956
Salcombe	JA Cook	1916	Silloth	JJ Johnstone	1956
Salcombe	JH Cove	1916	Silloth	AB Ramsay	1956
Salcombe	JA Cudd	1916	Skegness	M Hildred	1874
Salcombe	FW Cudd	1916	Skerries	A Anning	1873
Salcombe	A Distin	1916	Skerries	R Cochrane	1873
Salcombe	SM Distin	1916	Skerries	W Fitzpatrick	1873
Salcombe	PH Foale (Snr)	1916	Skerries	J Halpin	1873
Salcombe	PH Foale (Jnr)	1916	Skerries	J Kelly	1873
Salcombe	WJ Foale	1916	Skerries	P Reid	1873
Salcombe	WW Lamble	1916	South Shields	J Bone	1849 **
Salcombe	T Putt	1916	South Shields	J Burn (Snr)	1849 **
Salcombe	AE Wood	1916	South Shields	J Burn (Jnr)	1849 **

STATION NAME	NAME	YEAR	STATION NAME	NAME	YEAR
South Shields	L Burn	1849 **	Spurn Point	H Holmes	1855 **
South Shields	J Donkin	1849 **	Staithes	J Crookes	1888
South Shields	R Donkin	1849 **	Staithes and Runswick	G Hanson	1957
South Shields	J Marshall	1849 **	Staithes and Runswick	JR Baxter	1990
South Shields	T Marshall	1849 **	Stonehaven	E Balls	1849 **
South Shields	J Matson	1849 **	Stonehaven	A Rogers	1849 **
South Shields	J Phillips	1849 **	Stonehaven	J Brown	1874
South Shields	R Phillips	1849 **	Stonehaven	J Lees	1874
South Shields	W Purvis	1849 **	Stonehaven	J Leiper	1874
South Shields	R Shotton	1849 **	Stonehaven	A Main	1874
South Shields	W Smith	1849 **	Stromness	J Mowatt	1866
South Shields	G Tindall	1849 **	Stromness	G Campbell	1902
South Shields	G Tinmouth	1849 **	Sunderland	JH Davison	1910
South Shields	J Wright	1849 **	Swanage	W Brown	1895
South Shields	J Wright	1849 **	Teignmouth	T Chaffe	1898
South Shields	H Young	1849 **	Tenby	J John	1988
South Shields	J Young	1849 **	The Lizard	R Harris	1866
Southport	J Ball	1886	The Lizard	P Mitchell	1866
Southport	C Hodge	1886	The Lizard	N Stevens	1866
Southport	H Hodge	1886	The Lizard	JC Curnow	1976
Southport	P Jackson	1886	The Mumbles	J Jenkins	1883
Southport	T Jackson	1886	The Mumbles	W Jenkins	1883
Southport	B Peters	1886	The Mumbles	W Macnamara	1883
Southport	R Peters	1886	The Mumbles	W Rogers	1883
Southport	H Rigby	1886	The Mumbles	D Claypitt	1903
Southport	T Rigby	1886	The Mumbles	J Gammon	1903
Southport	T Rigby	1886	The Mumbles	G Michael	1903
Southport	J Robinson	1886	The Mumbles	DJ Morgan	1903
Southport	R Robinson	1886	The Mumbles	T Rogers	1903
Southport	T Spencer	1886	The Mumbles	R Smith	1903
Southport	P Wright	1886	The Mumbles	WG Davies	1947
Southport	F Rigby	1899	The Mumbles	WJ Gammon	1947
Southport	J Robinson	1899	The Mumbles	E Griffin	1947
Southport	W Robinson	1899	The Mumbles	WL Howell	1947
Southsea	E Main	1892	The Mumbles	W Noel	1947
Southwold	G Ellis	1858	The Mumbles	R Smith	1947
Southwold	Rev R Hodges	1858	The Mumbles	WR Thomas	1947
Southwold	J Ord	1858	The Mumbles	WRS Thomas	1947
Spurn Point	J Branton	1850 **	Torbay	FR Tucker	1940
Spurn Point	M H Welburn	1853 **	Tramore	T Crotty	1858
Spurn Point	J Combes	1855 **	Tramore	J Fitzgerald	1858

STATION NAME	NAME	YEAR	STATION NAME	NAME	YEAR
Troon	T Warren	1931	Whitby	R Gatenby	1877
Troon	J McCaull	1949	Whitby	S Lacey	1877
Tynemouth	J Grant	1864	Whitby	J Thompson	1877
Tynemouth	E Robson	1864	Whitby	J Pounder	1881
Tynemouth	RT Arkley	1872 **	Whitby	J Harland	1924
Tynemouth	J Watson	1872	Whitby	JR Dryden	1940
Tynemouth	J Wheatley	1872	Whitby	C Wale	1940
Walmer	E Young	1896	Whitby	D Harland	1955
Walmer	J Rich	1950	Whitehaven	T Farrell	1813 *
Walton and Frinton	C Bambridge	1911	Whitehaven	J Hailey	1881
Walton-on-the-Naze	F Batchelor	1889	Whitehaven	JW Henney	1886
Walton-on-the-Naze	J Downes	1892	Wick	A Bain	1857 **
Wells	F Abel	1880	Winchelsea	G Terry	1864
Wells	J Elsdon	1880	Winchelsea	E Robus	1882
Wells	RW Elsdon	1880	Workington	A Dunnon	1885
Wells	W Field	1880	Worthing	H Bacon	1850
Wells	W Green	1880	Worthing	J Belville	1850
Wells	C Hines	1880	Worthing	J Edwards	1850
Wells	G Jay	1880	Worthing	S Edwards	1850
Wells	C Smith	1880	Worthing	W Hoskins	1850
Wells	S Smith	1880	Worthing	H Newman	1850
Wells	J Stacey	1880	Worthing	J Newman (Snr)	1850
Wells	W Wordingham	1880	Worthing	J Newman (Jnr)	1850
Weymouth	Cdr J R Pennington Legh DSC	1944	Worthing	J Newman	1850
Weymouth	R H Treadwell	1944	Worthing	H Slaughter	1850
Whitby	J Pattinson	1841 **	Worthing	W Wicks	1850
Whitby	R Storr	1841 **	Worthing	G Riddles	1892
Whitby	R Walker	1841 **	Worthing	C Lambeth	1895
Whitby	J Wilson	1841 **	Worthing	EJ Burgess	1915
Whitby	C Collins	1861 **	Youghal	M O'Brien	1873
Whitby	J Dixon	1861 **			
Whitby	I Dobson	1861 **			
Whitby	R Harland	1861 **			
Whitby	M Leadley	1861 **			
Whitby	R Leadley	1861 **			
Whitby	G Martin	1861 **			
Whitby	J Philpot	1861 **			
Whitby	J Storr	1861 **			
Whitby	W Storr	1861 **			
Whitby	W Tyreman	1861 **			
Whitby	W Walker	1861 **			

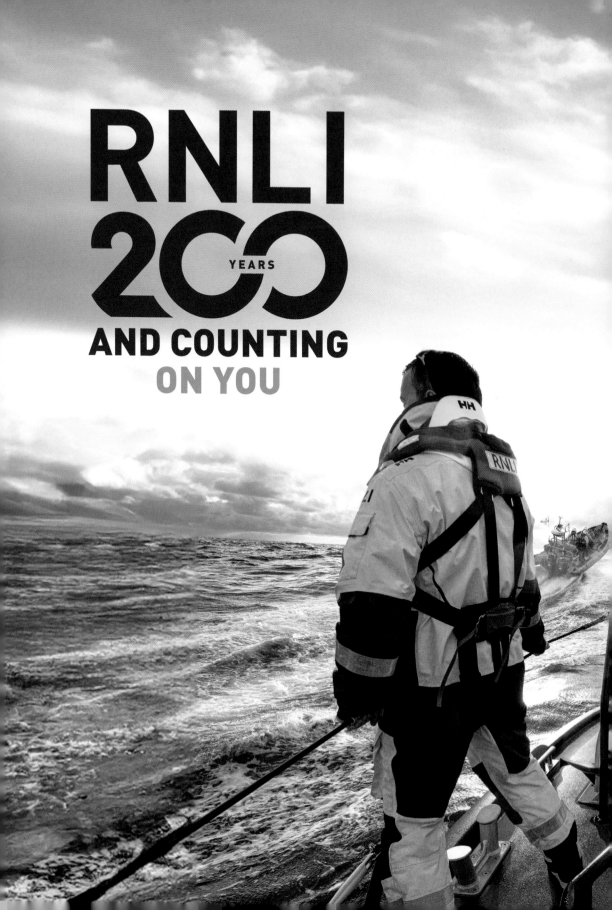

JOIN THE CREW!

However you get involved in the RNLI, you'll be a lifesaver too – because we depend on supporters, volunteers and fundraisers to power the charity.

**Find out how you can help
save every one we can at RNLI.org**

f Facebook.com/RNLI

▶ Youtube.com/RNLI

𝕏 X.com/rnli

♪ TikTok.com/@RNLI

in LinkedIn.com/RNLI

⊙ Instagram.com/rnli

PICTURE CREDITS

INDEX

Page numbers in **bold** denote illustrations.

A minimum of £8,000 from the sale of this book will be paid in support of the RNLI. Payments are made to RNLI (Sales) Ltd, which pays all its taxable profits to the RNLI, a charity registered in England and Wales (209603), Scotland (SC037736), the Republic of Ireland (20003326), the Bailiwick of Jersey (14), the Isle of Man (1308 and 006329F) and the Bailiwick of Guernsey and Alderney, of West Quay Road, Poole, Dorset BN15 1HZ.

HarperCollins*Publishers*
1 London Bridge Street
London SE1 9GF

www.harpercollins.co.uk

HarperCollins*Publishers*
Macken House, 39/40 Mayor Street Upper
Dublin 1, D01 C9W8, Ireland

First published by HarperCollins*Publishers* 2024

10 9 8 7 6 5 4 3 2 1

© RNLI 2024

The RNLI asserts the moral right to be identified as the author of this work

A catalogue record of this book is available from the British Library

ISBN 978-0-00-861305-1

Printed and bound in Latvia by PNB Print

This book is produced from independently certified FSC™ paper
to ensure responsible forest management.

Acknowledgements
The RNLI would like to thank the following people for their help in creating this book:

Agnieszka Bania, Amy Bratley, Mark Bolland, Alice Butler, Jessica Cselko, Alice Dewsnapp, Eleanor Driscoll, Mairéad Dwane, Lydia Good, Rachel Hanford, Chloe Hatipoglu, Sarah Hammond, Charlotte Hill, Pippa Hill, Vicki Lovegrove-Fray, Nigel Millard, Ashton Milton, Kara Neilsen, Isobel Noctor, Emily Scott, Jim Smith, Rory Stamp, Robin Westcott, Hayley Whiting, Nathan Williams, Catherine Wood, Jimmy Young